GARI MEACHAM

spirit hunger workbook

FILLING OUR DEEP LONGING

TO CONNECT WITH GOD

Six Sessions

ZONDERVAN®

ZONDERVAN.com/
AUTHORTRACKER
follow your favorite authors

We want to hear from you. Please send your comments about this book to us in care of zreview@zondervan.com. Thank you.

ZONDERVAN

Spirit Hunger Workbook
Copyright © 2012 by Gari Meacham

This title is also available as a Zondervan ebook. Visit www.zondervan.com/ebooks.

Requests for information should be addressed to:

Zondervan, *Grand Rapids, Michigan 49530*

ISBN 978-0-310-68822-8

Published in association with Books & Such Literary Agency, 52 Mission Circle, Suite 122, PMB 170, Santa Rosa, CA 95409-5370, www.booksandsuch.com.

Cover design: Greg Johnson / Thinkpen Design
Cover photography: Shutterstock®
Interior design: Matthew Van Zomeren

Printed in the United States of America

17 18 19 /DCI/ 20 19 18 17 16 15 14 13 12 11 10 9 8 7 6 5 4

CONTENTS

INVITATION

I love invitations. They make me feel like I get to be a part of something. So rather than call this an introduction or a meet-and-greet the author, I'd like to *invite* you to something—a chance to get gutsy with God.

Gutsy is my favorite word. It's the new *brave*, if you will. Yet, as admirable and adventurous as this word sounds, it's often more tempting to stay safe in my love for God rather than daring; cozy rather than courageous. Do my prayers reflect the desire I have to communicate with God? Do I listen for God, or do I talk right over him? What would happen if I truly abandoned myself to experience an adventure with God?

I found myself reading one of the psalms in which David cried out with a desperate longing for his Creator. Actually, his cry sounded more like moaning. Although I can cry and moan with the best of them, I was struck that the motive behind my moaning often centers on me, not my longing for God. It was this "aha" moment that inspired me to surge into a new way of engaging him. A gutsy way of praying and believing this God I proclaim to adore.

When I was a young girl, whenever someone did something fantastic we'd yell, "That took guts!" Privately, I always wished I could ask those people how they mustered up the courage to try things differently. How did they gather their wits about them and move ahead, regardless of the fear or cynicism that whispers, "You'll never change"?

We live in a time when there's never been more access to great material— books, magazines, webcasts, blogs, sermons, seminars. We seem to be either information gluttons or malnourished seekers. But the real question behind this glut of material is three simple words: *Are we changing?*

I want to do more than moan; I want to long for the God who can change me.

So, with an invitation filled with promise, adventure, and guts — I ask you to join me. Grab a coffee, sweet tea (my current favorite), or water with a bright-yellow lemon wedge. Sit down by yourself or with good friends, and enjoy this ride. I promise it will be anything but boring. I've often said that if you preach to me, I retain a portion of what was said, but if you walk alongside me, that's when I grow. We walk this path as fellow travelers, you and I, and I promise for the next six weeks we will grow together as we hike some rough terrain and meander in some lush meadows. At the end of this study I can't wait to say to you, "You've got guts!" — because that's what your life will reflect; a gutsy new way of loving our God.

Sweet Blessings!
Gari

HOW TO USE THIS WORKBOOK

The *Spirit Hunger Workbook* is intended for use with the *Spirit Hunger* video, sold separately. My book of the same name is also recommended as supplemental reading, but is not required to fully enjoy the study.

The main feature of the workbook is a five-day personal study for each session. This is a time when you can feed and fill yourself with God's Word and company. For those of you who crave even further study, I've included an optional "Going Deeper" section at the end of most days. Look at this section as a type of spiritual espresso where you can explore what we've covered that day in a bit more depth—like adding an extra caffeine kick to your Bible study!

Spirit Hunger is designed to be used in either group or individual settings:

FOR GROUP USE

If you're enjoying *Spirit Hunger* as a group, I've set up your time together a bit differently than what you may be used to. In weeks two through six, you will begin with group discussion questions that touch on the personal study you did individually the prior week. It's a starting point for groups and leaders, filled with questions you can mull over and linger around. Then you will watch a video teaching segment, approximately twenty minutes long, introducing the topic of the personal study for the following week. (The workbook includes an overview for all the video segments that highlights the main points as well as space to jot a few notes.)

In week one, because you will not yet have completed a personal study, you will start by viewing the video segment and then discussing the related questions. These questions will take you to the heart of *Spirit Hunger* and prepare you for the weeks to come.

I've also included a bonus week—week seven—so that you can get together to discuss the personal study from week six and end your study of *Spirit Hunger* in a time of prayer.

The material provided for each session should easily fill about an hour; if your group meets longer, I'm sure you'll put the additional time to good use!

FOR INDIVIDUAL USE

If you're not currently in a group, there's no reason you can't benefit from this study in your own personal devotional time (or perhaps with a good friend). Simply watch the video segments on your TV or computer and answer the group discussion questions on your own.

LET'S "EAT"!

I love sitting around a table after a meal talking, laughing, and telling stories. I hope you'll find this study to be like a great conversation after a meal. I can't wait to dine with you, friends, and although I'm not much of a cook—I am a lover of good talks, God's Word, and moments of clarity that fill our spirit's hunger to be fed. So with great anticipation, let's start our study.

spirit hunger
workbook

Session
One

HIDING, CONTROLLING, and MOCHA LATTES

Have you ever felt a gnawing inside, a tug of emotion that lingers with a sense of emptiness even though life seems full? Sometimes it grabs me at night when my mind finally settles after a full day; other times I wake with it—a hope that today will fulfill my heart's desire for something I can't quite name. This gnawing tug of possibility is our *Spirit Hunger*, the place inside us that longs to connect with God.

I wandered around for years wondering what that yearning was. Why I could achieve certain goals and still feel empty. Why I could be surrounded by people and still feel alone. Even after falling head over heels in love with my Savior Jesus, that wrenching desire can still overtake me like waves crashing on a rocky beach.

After running from, numbing, ignoring, stuffing, and analyzing this desire till I'm blue in the face, I've come to recognize the hunger pains of my spirit—the way it woos me back to the true filling it desires, an authentic and continual dining with God.

VIDEO TEACHING (19 minutes)

Watch the video. The main points are included here for you. Jot down additional notes if you wish.

The tone in many of the psalms is that of desperation, yet often we find ourselves committed but not desperate.

We long for things that make us uniquely women: nurturing; affirmation; to be noticed and heard—but there is a longing at the core of women's lives that bullies itself in front of all other longings: the longing to be in control.

This need for control came from the first woman, Eve. (Genesis 3:6)

What happened in the garden is referred to as a sin issue, but it was also a control issue.

Control has a muzzle. The muzzle to control is trust.

God taught women trust after their exodus from Egypt. In the wilderness they were only able to gather a day's worth of what they needed to sustain their families. They had to trust that God would provide tomorrow what he had today.

Our spirits long to trust God, not control him.

GROUP DISCUSSION (approx. 25 minutes)

Discuss the following questions related to the video you just watched.

1. What's the difference between a committed Christian and a desperate Christian?

2. Donald Miller, author of the book *Blue like Jazz*, says "The opposite of love is not hate; it's control." How does this definition change your view of control?

3. How were the events in the Garden of Eden not just a sin issue, but a control issue? (See Genesis 3:6.)

4. Gari mentioned the following descriptions in her list *"How to Know If You Have Issues with Control."* Can you think of others to add to the list?

   • Won't let anyone help in the kitchen or around the house, but then complains that if *she* doesn't do the chores, they won't be done right.
   • Uses nagging as a tool because if she doesn't nag, people won't budge.
   • Claims she wants a strong husband who leads, but criticizes when he tries to.
   • Exhausts herself trying to make everyone happy.
   • Tells other people how to drive, how to do things, and generally makes all the decisions and choices in the household.

5. How is trusting God a muzzle to control?

6. If our spirits long to trust God—not control him—how can we let go of control and practice trust?

PERSONAL STUDY

DAY ONE SWEET OR SASSY?

I've never been a coffee drinker. I know that's one step short of sacrilegious in a country that has a Starbucks on every corner, but a few years ago I found a drink that rivals anything I've ever wanted to suck through a straw—sweet tea. It may sound silly, but when I'm crawling into bed at night I actually get excited to drink a big tea the next day. I don't have many habits; as a matter of fact, God has taken me through some achy times exposing behaviors and compulsions that have teased my heart away from him. Thankfully, the sweet tea seems to be okay.

As I think about my physical longing for sweet tea, I'm reminded of what psychologists have known for centuries: Certain longings are universal to humanity. They begin when we are born and carry through our lives until we take our last breath. Much more important than sweet tea (although I may beg to differ some mornings) is our longing for nurture, attention, and affirmation. We long for filling and purpose; we long for intimacy—to be treasured and valued; and sitting at the top of the list is our longing to authentically connect with God.

Although these sound beautiful, like dainty flowers in a vase, we often have no clue what to do with these longings when they beg for attention they don't receive.

How did things get so messed up? When did the longings in our lives turn to hauntings? Why do these longings get tangled with counterfeit fillings?

I believe the answer to these questions can be found in the very first woman to walk the earth—Eve. I've always heard the story of Adam and Eve referred to as *the fall of man*, but I'd like to call it *the devastation of woman*, because what happened that day in the garden changed the face of women's hearts and longings forever.

Please turn to Genesis 3 and read verses 1–6. Write out verse 6 below.

The Bible says that after Eve ate of the fruit, she gave it to her husband and he ate too. There's no time frame given for how quickly he ate, but I have a hunch it wasn't immediate. The truth is Adam knew better, but I think Eve wore him down. Maybe it went something like this: "Adam, try this fruit that I've eaten; it's great!" If he looked at her with a raised eyebrow, I think she went for the nagging approach, "Adam (said with a bit of a whine), you really need to eat this. I'm serious. Eat!" If that didn't work, I think she coyly began to cry, "Why don't you want to do like I've done? Don't you want to share this special moment with me?"

Whether he ate to get her to be quiet, or he just didn't have the spine to stand up to her, *control* has now bullied its way onto the list of our longings. Prior to the "devastation of woman," the word *control* had never been uttered. Now it's screaming from the treetops.

To this day, it seems that women battle for control and men battle being cowards. Do you see any "control" issues lurking in your life? (Just so you know, it can come in the form of nagging, trying to make everyone happy, being bossy, or frantically trying to keep all your ducks in a row!)

I spent many years believing I didn't have a problem with control. I had so many other issues God had to deal with; control just didn't seem to be one of them. Until one day I realized that my issues with control were wrapped in a sweet package with a pretty bow, but were stinky and mildewed when I got them out in the light. Sometimes I feel like I'm two different women—the loving and kind me I'll call *Sweet Girl* and the controlling, manipulating me I'll call *Sassy Pants Girl*.

If you've never considered yourself a Sassy Pants, see if you can relate to some of these characteristics of a controlling woman. Check any that sound like you.

❑ Won't let anyone help in the kitchen or around the house, but then complains that if *she* doesn't do everything it won't be done right.

❑ Uses nagging as a tool because if she doesn't nag, people won't budge.

❑ Tries relentlessly to have everyone dressed perfect, acting perfect, and living perfect; but when something happens off her script, she yells or breaks down and cries.

❑ Claims she wants a strong husband who leads, but then criticizes when he tries to.

❑ Exhausts herself trying to make everyone happy and put out emotional fires.

❑ Tells other people how to drive or do things; always gives advice and opinions even when they aren't welcome; generally makes all the decisions or choices within the household.

❑ Charmingly says, "Whatever you want …," but then seethes when the choice isn't what *she* wants!

If you're aware of any other ways you attempt to control, note them here.

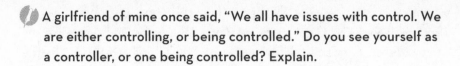 A girlfriend of mine once said, "We all have issues with control. We are either controlling, or being controlled." Do you see yourself as a controller, or one being controlled? Explain.

I remember one of the first times I experienced being mugged by control. My husband, Bobby, was a fresh face on the New York Yankees roster. After a few stints playing for them and being sent back to the minor leagues, it looked like he was going to be their starting shortstop for a while. So, in a blitz of excitement, I began looking for a place to live. In baseball life, the joke is — if you buy a home somewhere, you're then going to be traded, released, or sent back to the minor leagues. But I had no time for superstitious joking; I wanted a home! After looking at a total of three homes, I proclaimed to Bobby that I had found our dream house. It was formally a chicken farm that had been made over by a couple who spent most of their time sleeping on unfinished floors with spackle smeared over their faces. I fell in love with the place and began to concoct a plan to convince Bobby that we had to have it. After some heavy persuading (controlling), he reluctantly agreed, and we signed the contract. We lived in that house for eight years and, in all honesty, we loved that home; but I have to admit it had many drawbacks that, had I listened or planned more carefully, I could have avoided. Here were a few of our homeowner follies: the entire place had to be rewired (electricians found old gas holders from gas lamps when they opened up the walls); termites were eating away at the roof; the basement was filled with asbestos, and squirrels had chewed their way inside and created a "squirrel condominium" in our attic. Daily, Bobby would trap these hissing varmints with peanut butter spread on bread, and cart the trap off to a local park only to find out they were probably beating him back home with their honing devices set on our attic!

Several years later, as Bobby and I found ourselves sitting on the couch of a counselor talking through some pain that had swelled in our marriage, he mentioned the fact that many years earlier he didn't express his true feelings about that house. Although we had many happy memories there, he felt as if he should have moved us to a warm climate during the baseball off-season so he could keep his skills sharp. My persuasive sassy pants convinced him to buy that home; it makes me wonder how his career may have played out had we lived somewhere else.

Now that I've stepped on all ten of my toes, I promise to stop. But let me end our time today by saying this: control is the ultimate counterfeit of love. It's the secret adulteress to good intent. Like a robber hiding in a dark closet, control ambushes us. It gags us, and then surveys what it can take from our lives without us noticing we've been robbed.

We're going to circle this topic again tomorrow, but you'll be glad to know that control has a muzzle, an off-switch. We'll get to that important truth on Day Three.

GOING DEEPER (OPTIONAL)

For the next six weeks, I'd like to ask you to grab a blank notebook, journal, or your iPad—anything you can use to write out your thoughts and mental meanderings. We talked about how control is the counterfeit of love. I'd like you to go back to the initial longings we discussed at the beginning of Day One and create a list. On one side of your list, name the longings we've discussed; on the other side, name a counterfeit for that longing. I'll show you my list; feel free to change words or add words of your own.

LONGINGS	COUNTERFEITS
nurture	control
intimacy	distrust
purpose	bland insecurity
discipline	laziness or procrastination
treasured	trampled or ignored

After you've created your list, can you see areas of true longing that are being crushed by counterfeit substitutes? How have these substitutes crept into your life? Are there events that led you to these counterfeit places, or has it been like the slow drip of a faucet? How do you think God can change counterfeit longings to true spirit desires?

DAY TWO HIDING THINGS UNDER TREES

Sometimes I shake my head at the way I think I can hand God my Day-Timer and say, "Here, make it happen." Being married to a professional baseball player has ripped more pages out of my planner than I can recall. After moving forty-seven times in a ten-year span, I finally started to write my plans in pencil rather than scribbling them in permanent marker.

When Bobby and I decided we were ready to have children, it was like the wind of a whistling tornado bowled me over. I was consumed with trying to plan (control) the birth of this new little prince or princess we hoped to conceive. I pulled out a baseball schedule for the next year and plotted a good time to deliver a child. Not in spring training (too inconvenient), not in the middle of the season (we'd probably be in the pennant race), but how about the off-season? The winter months when baseball is dormant seemed the perfect time for our angel to enter this world. I told God about this perfect plan and asked him to come along if he'd like.

Much to my surprise, I got pregnant quickly; but with no regard to my plan, the due date of this baby was precisely in the middle of spring training. After a bit of bristling, I came to terms with the date and settled into dreams of a nursery and sweet gurgles. But after the first signs of spotting, no amount of bed rest could stop the inevitable loss of that sweet child. Bewildered and heartbroken, I asked God why he hadn't followed my plan.

A few months later, we were pregnant again. I was cautiously excited, and after my first visit to the doctor I realized this child's due date, May 26, was during the regular season. However, mid-May arrived and my doctor pushed the due date back to June 6. June came and went—no baby! I was seeing the doctor every day to be monitored for this child that didn't want to leave my womb. We finally welcomed our daughter, Brooke Nicole, to the world on July 3—smack in the middle of a heated pennant race, and almost two months after the date I anticipated her arrival. So much for trying to control God!

If you've ever felt like you've tried to corral God into your way of thinking, planning, or behaving—welcome to the sisterhood, sweet friends. It's comforting to know we're in good company. Many good women in Scripture struggled with control issues. Nothing thrills me more than seeing Bible women who are as messed up as me!

Sarah (originally Sarai) was a godly woman with major control issues. She's one of the few women physically described as gorgeous; married to a prominent man of wealth and stature, Abraham; it looked like they were a couple who had it all. But her heartache came in the form of infertility, and it was through this heartache she learned to trust God. Unfortunately, not before she made some huge mistakes as she tried to "help" God with his promises for her life.

Please turn to Genesis 16 and read verses 1–3. Note below how long Sarah and Abraham had lived in Canaan.

After ten years of waiting and praying, what was Sarah's plan to remedy God's delay?

The end of verse 2 contains a phrase that is "pregnant" with meaning. Please write verse 2 below, and note Abraham's response to Sarah's request.

Why in the world would Abraham agree to this arrangement? After all, wasn't he the one who heard God's promise for an heir with his own ears? Suddenly I'm reminded of the *control/coward* cycle we saw play out with Adam and Eve. Abraham knows better, but instead of standing as a protector, he lets the controlling whine of his wife dictate the events within his family.

The trouble with control is that whenever we manipulate circumstances to get what we want, it never fills us like we thought it would. Consider Sarah's response to getting what she wanted. Please read verses 4–6 and notice Sarah's sudden change of character.

With whom is Sarah mad?

Ultimately, she's now mad at her husband, her maid, *and* God! She's so mad that she's treating Hagar harshly. Hagar, who did nothing but follow Sarah's orders and become pregnant, is now the recipient of rude interaction and hateful drama. Hagar is so distraught that she runs away from the mess and has a powerful encounter with God.

Please read verses 7–13. Who visited Hagar in her painful running?

While there is debate about the identity of the angel of the Lord, the evidence suggests that it was an appearance of God himself. It's particularly significant that this is the first record of such a divine appearance. Think of it! God did not come as the angel of the Lord to Adam, Noah, Abraham, or any of the great men of Genesis. Instead, he came to an Egyptian slave woman.[1]

In verse 13 Hagar gives God a name. What does she call him?

✦ "The God who sees" is a beautiful description of God's interaction with his women. If someone truly sees us, they know us. Are you experiencing the loving look of God in your life, or are you feeling distant or unseen?

It seemed that Sarah and Hagar had peace for a while, or maybe they just stayed on different ends of the camp—but Hagar gave birth to a son named Ishmael. Even though it was Sarah's plan to raise this son as her own, she never seemed to bond with the boy—another reminder that manipulation rarely brings satisfaction. In God's time, Sarah finally became pregnant and gave birth to her beloved Isaac, but her struggles with control were far from over. At a party held for Isaac's weaning (think birthday bash for a three-year-old), she saw Isaac's older half brother, now around sixteen years old, taunting and teasing her son.

✦ Read Genesis 21:9 – 21. What does Sarah's "control rage" sound like in verse 10? Does it seem harsh to you?

✦ Hagar finds herself wandering in the desert again, but this time she's not alone—her teenage son is with her. Where does she leave him (v. 15) and why (v. 16)?

✦ Hagar can't bear to see her boy die, and as she is wailing and crying before God, who else is crying (v. 17)?

🍃 **Please write out verse 19 below, and underline what God did for Hagar physically.**

God opened Hagar's eyes! This is fascinating when we realize that the well of water was there all the time; she just didn't have eyes to see it. I wonder how often this happens in our lives. We're crying, wailing, begging God for help and the answer is right there; we just need him to open our eyes to see it. Financial heartache, relational pain, health issues, dead-end jobs, marital strife, loneliness, poor self-image—could it be that relief is near us and we just don't have the eyes to see?

Hagar did the only thing she knew to do with what she loved the most— she hid him under a bush, and then lifted her voice to God. What do you love the most in your life? What are you the most afraid of losing or letting go of? Typically, these are the areas we try to control. Can you list some of the things you hide under a bush? I'll get you started with a few of my own: my children and their futures, my husband's ever-changing job, my health, my schedule.

🍃 **Your turn:**

1.

2.

3.

4.

5.

6. Other:

I love God's words to Hagar after she has hid her son under a bush. *"What is the matter, Hagar? Do not be afraid; God has heard the boy crying as he lies there. Lift the boy up and take him by the hand, for I will make him into a great nation"* (v. 17).

Just when we think God isn't listening to our cries from our deserts and hiding places, he simply says, "Don't be afraid because I see you." Sweet friends, when God opens our eyes we see differently. Hagar was able to drink from living water, and then give to her desperate son from God's provision. Rather than control God, we can drink from him. He opens our eyes to a drink that satisfies and quenches our deepest thirst.

GOING DEEPER (OPTIONAL)

Scripture records the story of another man who was found under a tree. His name was Nathanael. Please turn to John 1:43–51. Notice where it was that Jesus saw this man. In your journal, write about what verse 50 means to you. How does it make you feel to know that Jesus sees *you* under your tree?

DAY THREE CONTROL'S MUZZLE

I have a deep love for schoolteachers. As a matter of fact, I think they have a job that ranks as high as the presidency with regard to impact and importance. Of course, because I taught school for fifteen years and was a national consultant for the Public Education Business Coalition after I left the classroom, I have an added sense of empathy and affection for those in the dusty trenches educating our youth.

I tried in every way to make my third-grade classroom stimulating. Bobby built a "tree house" that nestled in the corner of the room where kids could read. I had two life-sized trees that stretched from the floor to the ceiling, with branches blossoming fake flowers and leaves. Under these trees were wicker couches and patio furniture outlined with picket fences. Twinkle lights hung from the ceiling, casting a sweet glow on the room throughout the day. We called our room "the garden"—and it was my hope that we would grow and bloom there.

Yet no amount of decorating can replace kids' need to feel safe. I found that we needed space each morning for community building—a time for sharing, asking questions, and expressing worries. So we gathered on the floor with twinkle lights shining above. Kids would share things about their lives; they'd ask questions and pour forth their concerns. I would delicately weave assurance over their words—sick mommies and daddies at home, broken families, not feeling smart enough to pass a test— whatever they wanted to share that day was our launching point.

I have to admit that the control freak in me didn't feel I could give up the fifteen minutes in the morning this took; there were so many "important" things I needed to get to. But I quickly recognized that the days we didn't meet as a community seemed to unravel. Students would talk inappropriately, murmur, complain, and be just plain antsy. Eventually I put a name to what took place in our room in the mornings. It was a *verbal gushing*, and if I handled it right, our days held the promise of interaction and trust.

No one understood verbal gushing more than the Israelites. After Moses led them out of Egypt, they found themselves in a peculiar place. It wasn't the desert they were now wandering in that put them over the edge; I think it was their loss of control. In Egypt they were slaves, brutally forced into hard labor and unfair circumstances, but they were used to the routine of bondage. This new freedom in the wilderness was so unfamiliar it about knocked their control-loving socks off. Sadly, sometimes we cling to what we're used to, even when what we're used to stinks!

Please turn to Exodus 16 and read verses 1–4.

It's interesting that the wilderness between Elim and Sinai where the Israelites were wandering is called Sin. You don't have to remind me that the wilderness of Sin is truly a mean wilderness. My life has the scars and healed wounds to prove it. This desert area is described as a vast, desolate, hostile land of stone and sand — the perfect place to test and teach God's beloved how to trust.

What does the Israelites' verbal gushing sound like in verse 3? Write down the things they longed to go back to.

It's funny how a little hunger can throw us into a tailspin. To give up freedom for the sake of food or comfort seems ridiculous, yet it's exactly where we often find ourselves. I've learned my greatest life lessons from food. There's not one kind of behavior regarding food that I haven't pitifully participated in. Bingeing, purging, starving, overeating, sneaking, managing — you name it, I've done it. I've been told that my intense desire to control food stemmed from the fact that my childhood seemed so out of control. At least food was something I could handle. But I wasn't handling it at all; it was handling me.

When I was nine years old, a tragic car accident left my dad paralyzed from the neck down. Our family spiraled into despair as my dad and mom struggled to redefine their lives. Mom's anguish led her to some dark places with alcohol, and by the time I went to college I was carrying more baggage than an international airport. At first, food became my confidant; eventually, it became an adulteress that lured me toward death. One day in college, on the verge of taking my life because of anorexia and food-related heartache, I asked Jesus to heal me. I challenged him by saying, "If you're really real, change my life. You're the only hope I have." No one was pushing ideology or religion; it was just me and Jesus, and a plea to save me from my attempt to control my out-of-control life. That's the good news about control; the more we give it up to God, the more we feel secure. The more we release our tight grip, the more he can hold the very hands that have released whatever they were holding on to.

But the Israelites weren't convinced that God could hold their fears and worries; so they kept gushing.

🔥 **Please read verses 11–21. Write out God's dining plan for the Israelites, and then circle what he hoped it would prove to them (v. 12).**

🔥 **Quails in the evenings and a flake-like thing in the morning was God's response to their hunger. What was the Israelites' reaction to the flake-like thing that appeared like frost in the mornings (v. 15)?**

They were so perplexed by this provision they literally whispered, "What is it?" Have you ever asked God the same thing? Maybe you've prayed for something you really want or need: a cure for a health issue, a new job opportunity, healing in a relationship, direction with decisions or dreams. It's tempting to say to God, "What is this stuff laying on the ground of my life?" Just because we don't recognize the way God sends his provision doesn't mean he's not providing it! Sometimes we're looking for a golden loaf of manna—baked and browned to perfection—when God has provided flakes he's baking into a different type of loaf. Something we can't even imagine.

Moses answered their question with a confident assurance that God's in control. *"It is the bread the LORD has given you to eat."* Not only had God given them bread, he gave specific instructions as to how to enjoy it.

What did God instruct in verses 16–18, and how did the people's gathering of the manna play out?

The one who gathered much _____.

The one who gathered little _____.

Everyone gathered _____.

Moses boldly explained, "Don't leave any of it until morning." For the control freaks in the crowd, this was near impossible. I feel strangely connected to these women in the desert. At least in Egypt they could control what their family ate and what they wanted to stuff in their mouths. Now they had to gather each day only enough for the meals they needed, knowing that the next day they would have to trust God would provide all over again.

Tomorrow we'll talk about the way things get stinky when we try to hoard God's provision instead of trust him for it. In the meantime, I think pastor and author Mark Batterson got it right when he said, "We want a one-week or one-month or one-year supply of God's provision, but God wants us to drop to our knees every day in raw dependence on Him. And God knows that if He provided too much too soon, we'd lose our spiritual hunger. He knows we'd stop trusting in our Provider and start trusting in the provision."[2]

GOING DEEPER (OPTIONAL)

Most people have heard about the manna God provided in the wilderness, but before he provided manna he miraculously turned bitter water to sweet hydration. Read Exodus 15:22–27 and consider memorizing verse 26: *And he said, "If you listen carefully to the LORD your God and do what is right in his eyes, if you pay attention to his commands and keep all his decrees, I will not bring on you any of the diseases I brought on the Egyptians, for I am the LORD, who heals you."*

Ponder these questions: How can God take bitterness and turn it into something sweet? How does the Lord heal my diseases—both physical and emotional—with his provision?

DAY FOUR MAGGOT MOMENTS

I know the title of today's personal study may already have some of you gagging, but please stay with me. I promise we'll be out of this muck soon! Let's jump right into our Scripture.

 Please turn to Exodus 16 and read verses 19–21. What did Moses command, and how did the Israelites respond?

I can hear the sigh of every parent, leader, teacher, and coach—"Why don't they listen to what I say?" I can just picture Moses grumbling under his breath, "I'm about to pull my long beard out! Why do these people refuse to do what they're told?" It's one of the few times we see Moses get angry with the people. He was often frustrated, but now he's mad.

Maybe Moses was mad because the command seemed so simple: Just take what you need and trust God for what you need the next day. I'm tempted to mumble, "Those dumb Israelites, why can't they get it together and trust God?" But truthfully, I relate to their stumbling. I've been deeply in love with God for over thirty years, and sometimes my first reaction is still to control rather than trust.

 What was the result of trying to hoard the manna? Write out verse 20 below.

I wish I could have heard the shrieks inside the tents when women pulled the covers from their manna containers and noticed that the "manna" was squirming. I'd have probably dropped the container on the ground and run, only to have to return later and clean up smelly maggots from the floor of the living space.

Trying to outthink God always ends up foul, in some way or another. This need for control offers a fake comfort to the unsure circumstances of life. Control morphs into grown-up pacifiers. It's a "binky" I'll try to grab anytime I feel uncomfortable—replacing my true spirit hunger with momentary comfort or soothing.

If a pacifier's role is to soothe and calm, what type of pacifiers do you grab for? Here's a list that might help you get started: food, shopping (a woman at a shoe store told me yesterday she has over a hundred pairs of shoes, and doesn't even have a job ... she laughed at her predicament, but my heart was breaking for her), mirrors, full schedules, alcohol, excessive exercise, daily lists that can be checked off perfectly, hours of mindless TV, the thrill of intimate gossip cloaked in a prayer request.

Like every child who's ever loved a binky, a time comes when we need to let it go. Nothing seems more ridiculous than an adult walking around sucking a rubber nipple. But how do we really change? How do we move away from cherished habits (behavior ruts) to a new way of looking at things—a fresh way of behaving? The answer to this question lies in the heartbeat of two words: *trust* and *obedience*.

I know we've heard these words smack us upside the head for years, but I'm talking about falling in love with these words. Giving yourself over to them like a bride gives herself to a groom on their wedding night. If you allow yourself to be redefined by trust and obedience, the outcome will be stunning: a godly woman who trusts rather than panics, who loves rather than spews, who confidently wakes each morning with purpose and hope.

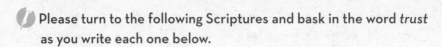 **Please turn to the following Scriptures and bask in the word *trust* as you write each one below.**

Psalm 4:3-5

Proverbs 3:5-8

John 14:27

Psalm 56:3-4

Trust is the muzzle to control. It's the off-switch to the constant drone of control's raspy whisper. The stately companion to trust is obedience. Trusting God does us no good if we're not willing to obey what he shows us in trust's sweet embrace.

I had always viewed obedience as a type of sacrifice—like I should receive some kind of spiritual applause because my obedience is such a chore. But I've come to view obedience as a gift, one I both receive and give. I reap the qualities of an obedient spirit (discipline, healthy choices, joyfulness, honesty) and hand my obedience to God as a love gift ("Here's my messy but obedient will, yours for the taking").

Oswald Chambers explains obedience with gentle clarity when he says, "The spirit of obedience gives more joy to God than anything else on earth.… When the love of God is shed abroad in my heart by the Holy Ghost (Romans 5:5), I am possessed by the nature of God, and I know by my obedience that I love him. The best measure of a spiritual life is not its ecstasies, but its obedience. To obey is better than sacrifice."[3]

May we lift the gifts of trust and obedience to God this day, and receive back the gifts of peace and clarity. It seems God can't be "outgifted" as he hands back far greater gifts than we courageously offer.

GOING DEEPER (OPTIONAL)

Why is trust one of the hardest things we ever do? Could it be that we are used to seeing trust trampled by humans, making it hard to find God trustworthy?

In your journal, do a trust survey of your life. Have there been key people who should have been trustworthy but weren't (parents, teachers, boyfriends, coaches, husbands, friends)? In what ways did their untrustworthy behavior make you skeptical of others, perhaps even God?

When you're done with your survey, read Isaiah 40:10–11 and 49:14–16 and write them next to your trust survey as a reminder of the type of trust you can count on with God.

DAY FIVE JESUS GETS WET

When I was in college, each summer I would return home to work at a local health club. One of my duties was to teach all kinds of aerobic classes. I know I'm dating myself here ... think big hair, leggings over tights, and disco music while we jumped around on a hardwood floor!

One day my boss informed me that he wanted me to teach water aerobics. *How hard can it be?* I thought, as I stood on the dry cement barking out commands to the ladies immersed in the pool. When the class ended, my boss called me aside and told me that to be an effective teacher I needed to get in the water with the ladies and actually do the class with them. I've never forgotten that lesson—and boy, was he right. Class attendance tripled, and so did my compassion for those I was teaching.

One of the things I love most about Jesus is that he was willing to be fully human—to experience the same fears, moods, pain, joy, and temptation to fill ourselves with things that don't draw us to God. Jesus does not teach us from the side of a pool; but rather he's in the pool with us, fully drenched with the struggles we face and the water we swallow just trying to stay afloat.

Please turn to Matthew 4 and read verses 1–11—the account of Jesus' testing by Satan in the wilderness.

The fact that Satan tried to tempt Jesus with "control issues" exhilarates me. It's like a fan blowing in my face when I'm drenched on a muggy day. Jesus not only understands this struggle, he overcame it!

After forty days and nights with no food, Jesus was vulnerable—and his vulnerability showed itself as hunger. Many books and sermons have been written and preached on this first temptation; and although I've had more than my share of struggles with this one, I want to focus on the following two enticements here (see more on the first temptation in "Going Deeper").

✏️ **Reread verses 5–7 and describe what you think Satan is after.**

In essence, Satan is saying, "You are in control of your own life. You are the boss of yourself. God won't let anything happen to you, so do as you please!" Can you imagine throwing yourself off the highest point of the temple just because you know God will protect you? In some ways, we've all done this. At times I've abused my body, nurtured thoughts that led me to dark places, withdrew when I should have pursued, and challenged when I should have submitted. All the while muttering, "God understands. He's got me covered."

✏️ **How is this kind of thinking a form of control?**

✏️ **Jesus stings Satan with the force of a hornet. What is his response to the absurd notion that we can test God?**

✏️ **Reread verses 8–10 and write verse 10 below.**

Jewish people have a word for bold assurance. It's *chutzpah* (pronounced "hoots-pah"), which has been described as utter nerve or sheer audacity that borders on obnoxiousness.[4] I hate to ever refer to Jesus as obnoxious, but I have to admit, we need to get more obnoxious in our dealings with Satan—because Satan certainly is obnoxious with us! Just like Jesus, we need to show some *chutzpah* when Satan lies to us.

Go back to the following three verses and write down the three words Jesus uses to start each of his responses to Satan's lies:

Verse 4: _____.

Verse 7: _____.

Verse 10: _____.

Imagine your life if you blasted Satan's lustful undertones with, "It is written!"

You are in control of your life. God doesn't really care what you do as long as you are a good person—No, it is written!

Go ahead and do whatever you want (eat gluttonously, drink excessively, sleep with people you aren't married to, live in a lazy state of procrastination), it's really no big deal—No, it is written!

Serve God; talk about him; pray to him; but don't pay attention to how he wants to capture every part of you with his healing breath—No, it is written!

What a jolt these three words are to a host of seductive temptations. I don't know about you, but I have a new vocabulary just itching to bounce off my lips. There's a new sheriff in town and his name is Jesus. I bet that etched across his badge are the words, "It is written." It's how he lived, how he spoke, how he loved, and how he died. "It is written" are the words that define Jesus.

I wonder what words define you. Look at the phrases and words below and check any that have a habit of oozing from your life:

❑ Whatever

❑ Maybe tomorrow

❑ What's the big deal?

❑ No one really cares

❑ Other: _____

Join me and add a new phrase to your life definition—*It is written*. Try saying it repeatedly today, and just for fun, notice how your day plays out a bit smoother.

GOING DEEPER (OPTIONAL)

I mentioned the first temptation Jesus faced was with food, but what intrigues me about this encounter is how Jesus refers back to the "flake-like thing" we mentioned in Day Three. Jesus quotes Deuteronomy 8:3 straight to Satan's repulsive face. Write this verse in your journal, and then describe the reason God allowed the Israelites to be hungry. Why did this statement fly in the face of Satan's lure for control? How can your spiritual hunger lead you back to the true source of satisfaction found in God alone?

Session

Two

ENGAGING GOD: from LONGING to PRAYER

I'm so excited we've made it through the first week. I feel bad when I start books with words like *control*, but now that we've trampled through some mud in our high heels, I think we're ready for a new pair of shoes. We may want to put on some comfortable (but stylish) walking shoes, because this week we're going to hike through the meadows of engaging God. We're going to move from a longing for God to the essence of communicating with him in prayer.

The easiest way we engage God is by prayer, but prayer is anything but easy. I spent years of my life wondering if I was missing something: questioning my skills, my motives, and my overall performance with prayer.

One day I was rummaging through a box I found that contained precious artifacts from my childhood. I have no idea why some things ended up in this treasure box—a box I decorated with ribbons, marker, and glitter. There were Girl Scout badges that I earned (and sometimes cheated my way to receive), a flowered tablet that had names of my future children scribbled on it (none of which I used when naming my three kids), a chipped ball from my neighbor's pool table, and a hot pink

bandana I used to wear as a headband. But tucked in one of the creases of the box I found a true treasure etched on a piece of yellowed notebook paper; it was a note I scribbled to God when I was eleven years old.

In words spelled out in black crayon, I laid my young soul bare. Tears washed away part of the note as the crayon blended pain and hope in a blurred splash of confused sorrow.

> Dear God,
>
> It's me, Gari. I hope you hear me because I don't know who else to write. I'm worried my dad will die since he stares at the walls and won't move much in his wheelchair. I hate having to feed him and then I feel guilty for not wanting to help more. I'm scared my mom will leave because she's so unhappy. I'm trying to take care of my little sister and brother, but I don't know if I can do a good enough job since I barely can take care of myself. Could you please show me if you are real? I hear people pray, but I don't understand. Could you show me you love me, if you really do? I can't stop crying, so I hope you can read these words on this page.
>
> Gari

As I read this priceless note, tears streamed down my face. I remember sitting at my desk writing it. Although I didn't know much about prayer then, I believe this was the first time I truly prayed. It was the first time I personally engaged God.

Real prayer isn't talking *at* God, but rather talking *to* him. It's a rhythm that pulsates between parent and child, friend and confidant, created and Creator. So with great anticipation, I invite you to explore this vast gift with me. To engage with the God who loves to respond to his children, even when they write in crayon …

GROUP DISCUSSION (approx. 25 minutes)

Discuss the following questions based on the week one personal study.

1. We've always heard what happened in the Garden of Eden referred to as "the fall of man," but how was it also "the devastation of woman"?

2. Do you feel as if you have two sides to your personality—Sweet Girl and Sassy Pants Girl? When do you see Sassy Pants start talking the loudest (when she's stressed, or intimidated, or tired, or battling PMS, or something else)?

3. In the story of Sarah and Abraham, how is Sarah's plan to conceive using her maid Hagar a form of control?

4. How do you react to this statement: "The trouble with control is that whenever we manipulate circumstances to get what we want, it never feels like we thought it would"?

5. God opened Hagar's eyes to see a well of water that may have been there all along, she just didn't have eyes to see it. Has God ever asked you to loosen your grip on something you love or are afraid of losing, so he can give you eyes to see things differently? Describe the experience.

6. In the midst of new experiences and freedom, the Israelites longed to go back to the place that held them in bondage. In our lives, why does going backward sometimes seem more appealing than moving forward?

7. Manna (the flake-like thing the Israelites didn't recognize) was the provision God gave the Israelites daily to teach them to trust. Has God brought an unexpected event, person, situation, or allowance into your life to teach *you* to trust? What is it?

8. What type of adult "pacifiers" do you tend to reach for?

9. How did Jesus stand up to Satan's lies regarding control? What were the words he repeatedly stated, and how do they hold the same power for us today?

10. If you have other insights or questions from last week's personal study, share them now as time permits.

VIDEO TEACHING (23 minutes)

Watch the video. The main points are included here for you. Jot down additional notes if you wish.

There are more books written on prayer than any other topic combined, yet we still often feel like we're not doing it right or not being heard.

Some of the reasons we feel stunted in our prayer life may include:

- We've gotten into a formulaic routine.
- We're trapped in meaningless repetition (Matthew 6:7).
- We don't have stamina or staying power.

Jesus understood this struggle as he explained to his disciples, *"The spirit is willing, but the flesh is weak"* (Mark 14:38). Thankfully, Jesus doesn't leave us in this weak state. He gives us instruction on how to pray.

The Maturity Continuum of Prayer (Matthew 7:7 – 8)

1. *Asking:* When we ask something of God, we're shifting to a place of intimacy with him. Sadly, many people stop at the asking phase because if they don't see an immediate answer, they think they're not being heard. God *always* answers prayer in one of three ways:

   - Yes … doors open and circumstances fall into place
   - No … when God answers no, it's for one of two reasons — protection or he has something better in mind for us
   - Not yet … but coming soon

2. *Seeking:* This is the confusing phase of prayer. We want quick and clear answers, but when we don't get them, Jesus says to keep seeking.

3. *Knocking:* The key to this phase of prayer is tenacity. Oswald Chambers defines tenacity as "the absolute certainty that what we hope for will transpire." This is the ultimate maturity in prayer — to keep knocking and engaging God even when things seem unclear.

PERSONAL STUDY

DAY ONE BURNT TOAST

Whenever I see a book with "Five Easy Steps" woven into the title, I want to run for the hills. I've lived long enough to know that most things in life can't be reduced to steps; and I've rarely found any steps to be easy. But year after year these titles sell, and I think I know why. We want formulas. We want a plan we can follow so we don't have to think. We want something that guarantees results.

I've seen hopeful prayer lives reduced to plastic formulas. Many women confide in me that after reading books on how to communicate with God, they still feel like they don't have an inkling of what to say to him unless there are scripted prayers included. Truthfully, I remember times in my own life when a formula sounded like a welcome retreat from the hard work of praying and not seeing! I've been told there are more books on prayer than any other topic in Christian literature, so why do we still wonder if we are doing it right? Why do we hear amazing answers to prayer in other people's lives, and wonder why our prayers smell like burnt toast?

The key to any formula is to repeat what is promised to bring the desired results. Formulas are based on the notion that if we repeat what we're told long enough, hard enough, and with just the right words, we'll get our answers. But Jesus isn't a fan of formulas. As a matter of fact, he speaks against this repetitive way of speaking to God, much like a mom would reject her kids uttering the same phrases all day long to get what they want.

 Please turn to Matthew 6 and read verse 7. What word or words does Jesus use to address this bad prayer habit?

One translation puts it bluntly, "And when you pray, do not keep on *babbling* like pagans, for they think they will be heard because of their many words" (NIV, emphasis added). Another exposes the fake nonsense by saying, "And when you are praying, do not use *meaningless repetition*, as the Gentiles do, for they suppose that they will be heard for their many words" (NASB, emphasis added).

In Jesus' day people seemed to pray for everything, but they had no personal knowledge of God. They recited prayers like a magical incantation, hoping that the god of this or that would respond with favor if they followed the right prescription of words.

It may be tempting to think this way of praying ceased after Jesus came on the scene. But it's still alive and well today. Even with a true knowledge of God, we can slip into a formulaic way of engaging him.

Have you ever felt like you were babbling or repetitive in prayer? Praying with your mouth, but having no real heart connection to what you're saying? Maybe you've prayed for a person or situation for such a long time that you numbly repeat the same things over and over without any real connection to God. Please write about it below.

(This is not to be confused with praying for the same things over a span of time. Persistence is a plus in God's column. I'm talking about praying with no real communion with God—engaging in the equivalent of empty chatter.)

The breathtaking thing about Jesus is how he understands and encourages us in our feeble attempts to pray. He explains things to us, mentors us, and cheers us toward a profound absorption in prayer. I used to think there was a type of prayer academy that if I were smart enough, I would graduate one day. But now I know that Jesus looks for people who are willing enough, not smart enough. He builds a sense of stamina in our wobbly prayers that takes us from distracted and disengaged to focused and zeroed in on his will.

Have you ever started to pray and suddenly all you can think about is your grocery list? On bended knees praying and your brain fixates on what you're going to watch on TV? I call this ADD prayer (Attention Deficit Devotion) and Jesus' best friends were pros at it.

Please turn to Luke 9 and read verses 28–36. Let's try to wrap our minds around this scene. Who did Jesus ask to join him on the mountain to pray?

What was physically happening while Jesus was praying? Describe his appearance and that of the Old Testament individuals who were with him.

Now write out verse 32 below.

For the love of Pete, how could you sleep when all this glory is transfiguring before you? Well, let's just say Peter and his companions had a stark awakening when they rubbed the crust from their eyes. Once awake, Peter rushed into performance mode as he told Jesus that it was good for them to be there, and he wanted to build something.

Only three times in the New Testament does God the Father speak — once at his Son's baptism, once on this hill, and once when Jesus asked his Father to be glorified. I believe he spoke on this occasion so Peter, James, and John wouldn't miss the point of this mind-blowing moment.

What does God say in verse 35?

Now, you'd think Peter, James, and John would never doze off again when in the presence of a praying Savior, but they were struggling learners with an ADD prayer life — and for those of us who understand this, it takes more than once to get the message! When Jesus gives them another chance to be upstanding prayer warriors, they again find themselves nodding off, except this time there was much more at stake.

Read Mark 14:32–36. What did Jesus instruct the disciples to do?

Circle the words that describe Jesus' state as he prayed that night.

Distressed	Relieved	Joyful
Troubled	Deeply Grieved	Overwhelmed

What does Jesus say when he comes back to his friends from this emotional wrestling in prayer (v. 37)?

While he's wrestling, they're snoozing. But Jesus doesn't yell at them or spank them verbally. He offers an explanation to this frustrating dilemma in verse 38. Please fill in the blanks below according to Jesus' words:

"The _____ is _____,

but the _____ is _____."

So there it is: the answer to why prayer isn't a cookie-cutter endeavor. Our spirits want to, but in our humanness we tussle to figure out how. No wonder we sometimes pray in a sleepy daze.

Thankfully, Jesus doesn't leave us in a yawning slumber. Tomorrow we're going to see how he boldly invites us to a vigorous way to pray. No need for a caffeine jolt—he effectively teaches us to toss our *burnt toast* way of praying for a fresh engagement with the bread of life.

GOING DEEPER (OPTIONAL)

Most people know about the first time the disciples slept in the Garden of Gethsemane as Jesus prayed. But I was shocked to see that this happened three times in a row! Please turn back to Mark 14 and read verses 37–42.

- Verse 37 is the first nap time for the disciples. What did Jesus tell them to do in verse 38?

- Now read verses 39–40. What was their response toward Jesus as he sees them sleeping a second time?

- Finally, what does Jesus say the third time he comes to them? How is he ready for what is to come? Did his time in prayer and anguish before God prepare him?

- Do you think the disciples might have been better prepared if they had been praying rather than sleeping (especially Peter)? Can you give examples of times you've wanted to pray, but ended up in a sleepy haze instead?

DAY TWO WORRY WALLOWING

A few years ago, I was the keynote speaker at a retreat on prayer. Nestled in a beautiful mountain lodge with expectant women—notebooks and pens in hand, ready to write down every word of utter wisdom I was about to impart—I found myself near tears. I was trying to teach on prayer, but was consumed with worry. It seemed that my life was exploding, and every thought led me down a seductive path of fretting instead of praying.

A few weeks earlier, Bobby and I were blindsided by the loss of his job. After wallowing in the minor leagues of baseball for sixteen years, traipsing the country from Oregon to Florida with low-paying jobs and humble positions, our dreams of making it back to the major leagues as a coach had finally come true. We landed our dream job, third base coach for the New York Yankees, and turned cartwheels (Bobby didn't, but I did!) when we realized that a decade and a half of prayers were wildly answered by our lavish God. I left my teaching job, certain that I could now pursue a twenty-year dream to write books and speak. But only a year later, we lost our dream job due to a bizarre set of circumstances that no amount of head scratching could explain.

During that time, I found myself sinking into puddles of worry faster than you could put on rain boots. Daily I would slosh around in the muck, repeating my worry chants like a rain dance:

- We're going to lose the house. We're drowning in college debt, bills, and life.
- My health is failing. These autoimmune diseases are consuming me.
- I'll never write books. I have to get a lousy job to help make ends meet.
- I guess it was too good to be true. I should remember that dreams are for the unrealistic, and from now on I need to be realistic.

As I stood before these women, it was as if God grabbed me in my drizzle and handed me an umbrella to keep the flood from engulfing me. The words "practice what you preach" have never held more meaning to me than during that weekend.

Thankfully, God took Bobby and me to some precious places of healing and hope during that wet season. It was through the loss of that job, and another stint in the minor leagues, that God brought us to a land of promise—Houston, Texas! Bobby ended up getting a major league job with the Houston Astros; and doors opened for me to write, teach, and speak that were wildly beyond anything I could have plotted or planned. It was during this time I learned to turn *worry prayer* to *asking prayer*; fretting into trusting; hand wringing into hope.

Have you ever wondered what worry really is? Some define it as anxiousness, or fear that sits in your head and festers. What does it look like in your life? What are you worried about today? Please write out your current "worry list" below.

In his well-known Sermon on the Mount, Jesus tells us not to worry. I know it's a little like telling a hungry child not to eat, but he really means it. "Don't worry!" Please turn to Matthew 6 and read verses 25–33. Write verse 27 below.

Jesus says we can't add one single hour to our lives by worrying, so why do we waste so many hours in a fretful state of anxiety? One of my Bible translations entitles this chapter in Matthew, *The Cure for Anxiety.* That's a gutsy promise offered by Jesus. I wonder if we have the guts to believe it.

Let's take these verses apart and wear this "No Worries!" label like a clever T-shirt. Note these truths:

- The same God who created life in you can be trusted with the details of your life. (v. 25)
- Worrying about the future hampers your efforts for today. (v. 26)

- Worrying is more harmful than helpful. (v. 27)
- God does not ignore those who depend on him. (vv. 28–30)
- Worry shows a lack of faith and understanding of God. (v. 32)
- There are real challenges God wants us to pursue, and worrying keeps us from them. (v. 33)
- Living with our eyes on God rather than circumstances keeps us from being consumed with worry. (v. 33)[5]

Which one of these statements resonates with you? What's happening in your life that makes it resonate?

Thankfully, Jesus doesn't proclaim, "Don't worry!" and then leave us on our own to figure it out. In a brilliant transfusion of faith, he leads us from a place of worry to a haven of hope. This hope is propelled by *asking* in prayer, rather than *fretting* in despair.

Turn to Matthew 7 and read verses 7–11. Then fill in these blanks:

If we ask, _____.

If we seek, _____.

If we knock, _____.

Jesus gives us a prayer continuum that can take us from wobbly toddler to steady adult if we have the courage to engage it. I often say, "If asking starts us in prayer, seeking confuses us; and knocking just plain irritates us!" Believe me, many a time I've gotten stuck at asking—wondering why God doesn't deliver on my tiny prayers that often are forgotten a second after they float from my mouth. They're not forgotten by God, of course; but they're forgotten by me, on to the next thing …

To ask God for something shifts us to a place of intimacy with him. It's a vulnerable place. Many people stop at the asking phase when they don't see an immediate answer, thinking God is either irritated by them or ignoring them, neither of which is true.

But when Jesus said to *ask*, he didn't follow it with a disclaimer. There's no fine print to decipher. The invitation is the same to anyone who will try it: simply ask.

 To ask is defined as making an appeal; to beg or inquire. Let's look at some of the ways this word is used in Scripture. Please write the verse beneath each reference.

Psalm 27:4

James 1:5

Proverbs 30:7 – 8

John 14:14

With humble assurance, we ask — we beg — we inquire. We won't stop until we receive, because this is the way Jesus presented his cure. Ask, don't worry ... and you *will* receive.

GOING DEEPER (OPTIONAL)

The disciples wanted to make sure they got this prayer thing right. After seeing Jesus praying, one of the disciples was prompted to ask Jesus to teach them to pray. This launched the famous model, *The Lord's Prayer*. Though we may have memorized this as a youth, repeat it daily as an adult, or have forgotten it altogether, we still have much to learn from it. Most scholars believe Jesus wasn't saying, "Pray these words exactly," as much as he was saying, "Have this attitude or approach to prayer." Please read his words in Luke 11:2–4 (NASB) and then write them in your journal:

> *Father, hallowed be Your name. Your kingdom come. (v. 2)*
>
> *Give us each day our daily bread. (v. 3)*
>
> *And forgive us our sins, for we ourselves also forgive everyone who is indebted to us.*
>
> *And lead us not into temptation. (v. 4)*

Now, place the following words next to the verses you think they apply to:

- Blemishes
- Provision
- Protection
- Worship
- Outward action

For those of you (like me!) who want to know the answers, here they are. (Blemishes: v. 4; Provision: v. 3; Protection: v. 4; Worship: v. 2; Outward action: v. 4)

This model of prayer came right before Jesus launched into his discussion around asking, seeking, and knocking (Luke 11:9). The Lord's Prayer is really about our *position with him*. His instruction in Luke 11:9 is really about *our petitioning of him*. How do they differ?

DAY THREE PRAYER GRIT

I hate to wait for things. I hate stoplights, lines at my favorite places, waiting for food to cook when I'm hungry. It's embarrassing to admit, but waiting is like watching my hair grow—slow with unnoticeable results until I see a line of gray requiring my hairdresser's magic touch.

I heard a comedian share his amazement that cell phones give us so much information thanks to the satellites that bounce the signals back to earth. He told a story about some teens he heard talking at the mall as they gathered around their phones. One of the teens was frustrated because her phone was taking a few extra seconds to load some information. On and on the girls moaned, until finally he said, "Give it a break. It's going to space!"

I don't think I'll ever talk to my phone rudely again. The truth is, I know that one of the fruits of the Spirit is patience, but I find myself wanting to throw unripe fruit in the trash because it's taking too long to get sweet!

When Jesus tells us to ask, seek, and knock, he's really inviting us to a seminar on patience. It's in the seeking phase of prayer that we learn to quit wiggling and get serious. This is the confusing phase of prayer where we want quick and clear answers, but don't seem to get them. Jesus said that those who seek will find, but that's the rub—if you don't keep seeking, you won't find anything but disillusioned faith and worn-out prayer chants.

I remember a time when God ratted out my immature seeking and taught me to pray with grit I never knew I had. When Bobby and I had been married ten years, I began to feel that something wasn't right. I chalked it up to the forty-seven moves we had endured and the ups and downs of a volatile career that left us waving good-bye to friends and teammates more times than I could count. With three small kids and another apartment in a new state, we were exhausted, but I knew this was more than being worn-out. The Holy Spirit began to purge Bobby of some dark secrets as he shared with me his struggle with infidelity and lies. I quickly plunged into the depths of despair as I begged God to give me answers.

During the months that Bobby and I were separated, one day after work I asked my sitter if she could stay a little longer. I drove to the foothills and crumbled beside a clear stream of water. Bible in hand, I began to seek God like a woman crawling through a hot desert. "Will our marriage survive? Can I ever trust this man I love again? What about our kids, finances, and all the Bible studies I lead—will I ever feel restored?"

I know that many of you are facing your own crumbling times: seeking answers to questions that seem impossible or too painful to put into words. Failing health, marital strife, abandoned families, betrayed hearts, crushed dreams, the loneliness of loss, kids making poor decisions, overcome by habits or addictions. I could go on and on as I think of God-seekers who struggle with real issues, yet trust a real God.

How do we seek so that we'll find the treasures God has for those who bravely stick it out? The main thing to remember is there's no time frame for your praying. When you seek, it may take days, months, or even years before you'll find. That's the beauty of the seeking stage: the stories God etches over your life along the way.

When I'm in the seeking phase of prayer, many things can seem unclear, so it's helpful to remember four things God makes *crystal clear* in his Word.

1. *God Is a God of Redemption*

 **Please turn to 2 Peter 3:9 and write it below.**

If you've been praying for years for someone to know God or to mature with him, you can be sure that God wants this seeking prayer answered as badly as you do. Don't give up! Keep praying!

If certain persons come to mind as you're reading this, write their names below as a reminder that your seeking will result in *their* finding.

2. We Can Be Free

 Please turn to John 8, verses 32 and 36, and write them below.

Have you been seeking freedom in prayer? Maybe there's a habit that engulfs you, or someone you love, and it seems you'll never be free from its grip. Overeating, compulsive behavior with food and dieting, drinking too much on a regular basis, drugs or other chemical dependencies, verbal assaults, yelling fits, bitter wounds that won't heal. I wish I could hold you in my arms and whisper these words in your ears: "You can be free."

The reason I say this with such assurance is that I have been bound in the cells of dark prisons, tugging and yanking at the chains, unaware of the key hanging within arm's reach outside the cell door. Jesus breathes the words of freedom that unlock our chains: "You will know the truth, and the truth will set you free." If he didn't mean it, he wouldn't have said it. We can be free, and it's those who seek freedom that find its restful embrace.

 Are you in need of freedom today? Is there someone you love who needs this seeking kind of prayer over their lives? Please write about it below.

3. We Can Have Peace

 Please turn to John 14:27 and write it out below.

Circumstances may shift, but God doesn't. Even in the midst of confusing and difficult situations, we can have a peace that the world doesn't understand. It flies in the face of reason that we can feel calm when a storm is raging around us, but seeking prayer leads us to this calm. We may not get immediate answers, but peace is the balm God rubs over our achy prayer muscles when we don't yet have the answers we seek.

 How is peace a by-product of prayer? Do you believe prayer can bring peace even when circumstances don't quickly change?

4. We Don't Have to Be Afraid

 Turn to Psalm 145:18–19 and write these verses below.

One of the by-products of the seeking phase of prayer is fear. When we seek and don't find, we often fall into fear's grasp. But God says that he hears us when we cry out to him, and at no time is our crying louder than when we're afraid.

Are you afraid of something? What seems to push you into this state of fear? How can seeking in prayer give you the confidence to keep going rather than shrink back?

Seeking takes grit. I love this word. It's so short and to the point. Grit means determination, fortitude, perseverance, and bravery. I have learned to grab this word and hang on to it with white knuckles, because it has changed the way I pray.

A couple pages back, I left you with a picture of me bawling my eyes out before the Lord beside a creek. After asking God if our marriage could endure the garbage that had been heaped upon it, I felt as though I saw a vision of another wedding. It was my husband and I, reciting new hope and promises to one another before God. I also saw us helping other men and women trapped by their secrets and lies. I wasn't sure if I was just "wishing" these things to be true, or if they were signs of encouragement from God, but I kept praying and seeking as if my life depended on it, and actually, I know it did.

A year later, my husband and I stood before a pastor, just the two of us, and renewed our vows. New rings and new hope filled the little chapel with glory. But it wasn't until fifteen years later that we stood before a gathering of a thousand people and shared our story of infidelity and healing. The effects of that speaking engagement continue to shock us as men and women have courageously revealed secrets and experienced a revival of love and new life they never dreamed possible.

So, with deep hope, we seek in prayer. The hope isn't centered on getting the answers we need as much as on the God we pray to for the answers. Sweet friend, be open, be authentic, and be ready—because seekers become finders in the kingdom of God.

GOING DEEPER (OPTIONAL)

In the seeking phase of prayer, I find it helpful to focus on various Bible images of God that visually connect me to him. Tricia McCary Rhodes has compiled two wonderful lists of images we can pray through while we're seeking.

Images of God from the Psalms

- A shield—Psalm 3:3
- My hiding place—Psalm 32:7
- God who works wonders—Psalm 77:14
- My fortress—Psalm 18:2
- Avenger of evil—Psalm 99:8
- Father of the fatherless—Psalm 68:5
- Holy and awesome—Psalm 111:9

Pictures of Jesus from the New Testament

- The good shepherd—John 10:1–16
- Silent when accused—Matthew 26:62–63
- The consoler—John 14:1–3
- The great physician—John 5:1–9
- The water of life—John 7:37
- The lamb—Revelation 17:14[6]

Pick two or three of these images and read the related Scriptures as prayers several times today. You may want to write them on cards or sticky notes to remind yourself that your seeking is a proactive state of prayer. It's a powerful way to engage God and to know your grit is growing!

DAY FOUR TENACIOUS KNOCKING

Yesterday I told you that I love the word *grit*. Although I do love this word, I sometimes wish the grits God had in mind looked more like a Southern side dish smothered in butter and honey. Unless I'm mistaken, prayer grit isn't smothered in anything but courage, and no amount of melted butter can make it go down easier. You have to stand up and stick with it … period.

I'm also obsessed with another word that has redecorated my mind toward prayer—and that's *tenacity*. I use this word when I speak, when I teach, when I pray, and when I silently think about God. Oswald Chambers defines *tenacity* as "the absolute certainty that what you hope for will transpire."[7]

Can you remember the last time you prayed for something with absolute certainty? A time you knew that what you hoped for would transpire? This is the knocking phase of prayer—a season of tenacious banging on doors.

Earlier, I mentioned that asking starts us in prayer, seeking confuses us, and knocking just plain irritates us! I believe the reason that it's irritating is we feel like we're spitting in the wind. We pray and pray … and nothing changes. We cry out, "God, are you hearing me?" Or worse, we mumble to ourselves that maybe prayer isn't really effective. We don't want anyone to hear us though, because questioning prayer would be mutiny in church circles. We're always told to pray, but nobody ever explains what happens after you do pray and don't see anything change.

I'd like to address this mutiny head on. God answers every single prayer you utter—every single one, with no exception. Here's how he answers:

- **Yes**—We pray and things happen. Circumstances make sense and fall into place gracefully. I saw this kind of prayer beautifully a few years ago when we put our home on the market to sell. We had tried to sell it three years earlier, but it sat and sat. This time was different; we knew God was taking us to a new place; and the house sold in four days.
- **No**—I realize we don't like to be told no, but God answers no for one of two reasons: either he's protecting us from something, or

he has something better in mind. "No" is actually a good answer, because it's always for our good, not to make us miss out on things we want. I think back to some of the things I thought I wanted (jobs, homes, boyfriends, husbands) and I'm appalled to imagine my life if God hadn't protected me!

- **Not yet … but coming soon**—When God says "not yet," there's a hopeful reason behind it. Sometimes we aren't ready for the new change he is about to bless us with. He may want us to continue to trust, seek, and knock just a bit longer so that our faith is unshakable for a future experience we may encounter. Sometimes he says "not yet" because we haven't dealt with a lingering sin that continues to lurk in the shadows of our lives. I've talked to so many young women desperately praying for a godly husband—and yet they continue to sleep with multiple partners, or act as if they're married to a man without the commitment of marriage. Sometimes the biggest obstacle to our prayers is us—not God!

Other times, you may be right in the heart of God's will, and still your prayer yearnings go unanswered. "Coming soon" is God's whisper to you. Bobby and I prayed for sixteen years that he would get a major league coaching job. Sixteen years of learning, persevering, and tenacious knocking. God was not answering no, as I sometimes misunderstood. He was saying, "Coming soon." I'm so glad we kept praying and knocking!

🌱 **Considering the three ways God answers prayers, do you see yourself in any particular stage of an answer? Please write about it below.**

Elizabeth is one woman in Scripture who understood what it meant to knock. Although most people know her as the mother of John the Baptist, after today I hope you also remember her as a tenacious lover of prayer.

Ⅰ Please turn to Luke 1 and read verses 5–7. What were Elizabeth and her husband, Zechariah, like spiritually?

Ⅰ What was their ultimate heartache?

Ⅰ Often, it's our ultimate heartache that becomes the jewel of tenacious prayer. Please read verses 8–13 and note Zechariah's reaction to the angel Gabriel.

Ⅰ In verse 13, after Gabriel assured Zechariah that he didn't need to be afraid, what did he specifically say to Zechariah that indicates the kind of "knocking" prayer he and Elizabeth had engaged in for years? Please write it below.

"Your prayer has been heard" might have been the sweetest words Zechariah ever heard. Because we know he and Elizabeth were advanced in years, or in easier language … old, we know they had been knocking on this door for a long time.

Ⅰ If you, too, have been praying for something for a long time, how does this encourage you to trust that God does hear?

⚘ **What was Zechariah's response to Gabriel and Gabriel's reaction to that response in verses 18 – 20?**

Although Zechariah was aware that he was part of something supernatural, his faith in what God could do was limited — so, in a comical turn of events, Gabriel made him silent for the next nine months. If we can be honest with each other, ladies, how many of you would love it if your husband didn't speak for nine months? I bet many of you are secretly saying, "Glory!" It's okay; no one will see this page of your workbook!

⚘ **Next, let's see how Elizabeth responded to God's answer to her knocking prayer. Read verses 24 – 25 and write her words in verse 25 below.**

This was a woman who recognized favor and grace. She didn't walk right by it; she rolled around in it!

The next time we meet Elizabeth it's about seven months later when her young relative Mary knocked on her door.

⚘ **Please read verses 39 – 45. What do we know about Elizabeth from verse 41?**

When someone is *filled with the Holy Spirit*, he or she acts differently. Notice Elizabeth wasn't threatened by Mary and the position of her son. She was completely whole and satisfied with the work God was doing in her own life … no need to compare it to Mary's life.

Notice that she built Mary up instead of feeling as if Mary were intruding on her pregnancy. There's no scent of jealousy, competition, or baby drama ("*my* pregnancy is harder than *your* pregnancy")—just a loud and excited exchange between two lovers of God who know something about tenacity. Elizabeth learned tenacity from years of prayer regarding her biggest loss: not being able to mother a child. And Mary would learn tenacity as she raised the Son of God, confused at times by the glory of this baby she nursed, and one day worshiping him at the foot of a cross.

🍃 **Please read verse 56 and note how long Mary stayed with Elizabeth.**

If you do the math, Mary was probably at her cousin's home during her own first trimester of pregnancy, and helped usher Elizabeth through her last trimester and the birth of her son, John. Can't you picture these women talking, praying, walking, cooking, and knitting booties for their boys? Isn't it so like God to give us time with just the right person before we have to face hard things? Things like birthing a child when you're old or going home to tell your fiancé you're already pregnant.

🍃 **Briefly thank God for your own times of refuge …**

How's this for an illustration of the tenacity we should associate with prayer? Dr. Ted Engstrom tells the story of three Korean workmen, laboring in China in the 1880s. They heard the gospel of Jesus Christ and were never the same. Soon they conspired about how to get the message of Christ into their own country, an action forbidden by the government. They drew straws to see who would have the privilege of bringing the gospel into Korea.

The first man buried the Bible into his belongings and headed to the border. There he was searched, found out, and killed. Word reached the others that their friend was dead. The second man tore the pages from his Bible and hid individual pages throughout his luggage. He, too, made the long trip to the border, only to be searched and beheaded.

The third man grew more determined than ever to succeed. He ingeniously tore his Bible apart page by page, folding each page into a tiny strip. He wove the strips into a rope and wrapped his baggage in his homemade rope. When he came to the border, the guards asked him to unwrap his belongings. Finding nothing unusual, they admitted him.

The man arrived home, untied the rope, and ironed out each page. He reassembled the Bible and began to preach Christ wherever he went.[8]

Knocking prayer — filled with the absolute certainty that what we pray for will transpire. May we knock on doors today ... even doors that seem slammed shut and locked.

GOING DEEPER (OPTIONAL)

After the birth of John, we don't hear about Elizabeth again. But even after delivering him, her strong character and tenacious spirit are evident. Read Luke 1:57 – 66 and notice verse 60. When Elizabeth said, "He is to be called John," she stepped on the toes of the religious and cultural establishment. Most boys were named after their fathers, but her boy had a predestined name, one that came from years of knocking. I don't think her knocking stopped there. Given the type of life her son would live, she probably continued banging on doors for the rest of her life. Do you see an area of your life that may qualify as a "lifetime" of knocking? Write about this knocking in your journal or the margins of your workbook.

DAY FIVE PRYING PRAYER

There's a type of seeking and knocking that pushes itself into its own category. It's prayer that wrenches from a gut cry to God in a language that mingles praying and crying. I call this type of prayer *prying*. Maybe you can relate. The praying and crying are so entwined that Kleenex and moans are one.

The last time I recall prying was Super Bowl Sunday 2011. We received a call from our oldest daughter's friend in San Francisco. She was talking in a panicked whisper, trying to explain that Brooke had been missing for over twenty-four hours after vanishing from a wine bar they had been to the night before. Without a trace, and no cell phone response, Bobby and I began talking to investigators and police. We called our son in Colorado and daughter in Atlanta, and decided the whole family needed to convene in California. When Bobby and I looked at each other in the middle of this frenzy, we fell face first onto the floor and *pried*—pouring out our anguish and fear to the God we loved and trusted.

Brooke was eventually found, safe in a hospital—but our spirits had endured a beating. When painful news hits, or a confusing circumstance smashes through the window of your life, the sanest thing you can do is pry.

There's a story in the Bible that exposes the humanity of Jesus in a compelling way. It's a window into the heart and emotion of the man we call Savior.

Jesus' cousin John the Baptist had been imprisoned by the nasty tetrarch Herod. Shortly after his imprisonment Jesus was delivered devastating news.

🖊 **Please turn to Matthew 14 and read verses 1–12. How do you think the conversation mentioned at the end of verse 12 went? What do you think the disciples said to Jesus as they explained this horrific murder?**

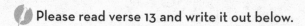 **Please read verse 13 and write it out below.**

If we could see Jesus floating in this small boat in a lonely cove, I believe we would see him *prying*. Fully God and fully man, ingesting the pain of loss and the heartache of surrender to circumstances that rage against making sense. One of the things I love most about Jesus is his understanding of struggle and sorrow.

Please turn to Isaiah 53:3 and write the first two phrases of this verse below.

"A man of sorrows, and acquainted with grief" (NASB)—now there's someone I can trust. The problem with sorrow and struggles is that I want to avoid them. I don't ever want to hear bad news. I don't ever want to go through difficult times or confusing situations. Do you?

I used to share with my students a short story that talks about struggles and sorrows of life. See if you can relate.

Struggles in Life

One day a small opening appeared on a cocoon. A man sat and watched the butterfly for several hours as it struggled to force its body through that little hole. Then it seemed to stop making any progress. It appeared as if it had gotten as far as it could and it could go no further. So the man decided to help the butterfly.

He took a pair of scissors and snipped off the remaining bit of the cocoon; the butterfly then emerged easily, but it had a swollen body and small, shriveled wings.

The man continued to watch the butterfly because he expected that at any moment, the wings would enlarge and expand to be able to support the body which would shrink in time. Neither happened! In fact, the butterfly spent the rest of its life crawling around with a swollen body and shriveled wings. It never was able to fly.

What the man in his kindness and haste did not understand was that the restricting cocoon, and the struggle required for the butterfly to get through the tiny opening, was life's way of forcing fluid from the body of the butterfly into his wings so that it would be ready for flight once it achieved its freedom from the cocoon.

Sometimes struggles are exactly what we need in our life. If we were to go through our life without any obstacles, it would cripple us. We would not be as strong as what we could have been.[9]

What happens if we aren't allowed to struggle? What changes if we try to sidestep pain?

There's another friend in Scripture who most likely *pried* himself to sleep night after night in a lonely prison cell. Thrown into jail because of a needy woman prone to lies, Joseph found himself in the center of circumstances that didn't make sense (and this wasn't the first time!). I know I'm asking you to read a lot today, but his story is so rich with struggle. Bobby and I named our son after this man; that's how much I admire his seeking and knocking in the midst of pain.

Please read Genesis 39, and focus on verses 19 – 23. Unfair life events — betrayals, abandonment, harsh words or lies, letdowns — are potentially devastating and can keep us stuck in a spiritual funk. How did Joseph's time in prison refine him?

As cozy as this may sound, it's still jail — and often in Joseph's day people would spend the rest of their lives imprisoned, with no hope of ever being released. Even after his former jail mates promised to remember him, Joseph was forgotten (Genesis 40:23).

How was Joseph's imprisonment like the butterfly squeezing to be free of a restricting cocoon?

Is there an area of your life that feels squeezed? How have you been tempted to cut open the cocoon so you can squeeze through?

Sweet friend, God will use every moment of squeezing, struggle, and pain to strengthen you and me for the glory our lives will reflect once we're out of the cocoon. May we keep prying and believing, as our wings are made ready to fly.

Session *Three*

WHISPERS and SCREAMS: HOW DO WE PRAY?

Prayer is like a frozen yogurt shop. Vanilla, dark chocolate, raspberry, key lime pie, cheesecake, tart, peanut butter, red velvet—these were some of the flavors I saw last night as I walked into my favorite yogurt joint. Grabbing a bowl, I began to labor over my choice. Don't even get me started on the toppings! Prayer is like this—so many ways to talk to God—sometimes sweet, sometimes tart, sometimes plain, sometimes edgy, and sometimes a mixture of flavors that don't seem to fit, but end up tasting good once they go down.

Sometimes our prayer is whispered as light as a breath. Richard Foster calls this Breath Prayer.[10] Prayers not more than seven or eight syllables rise from our hearts and through our mouths: "Precious Jesus, remove my fear." "Show me your love, Lord; show me your love." "Give me your eyes, Jesus; help me to see." Like the rhythm of a breath, these prayers calm and assure us as we utter them.

Other types of prayer seem to stir up a hornet's nest. Prayers for change, direction, deliverance, and hope can buzz through the bland covering of silence with a sting of determination and resolve.

Trying to name types of prayer is a bit like naming blades of grass. How do we begin to distinguish the vast ways we encounter God? For our purposes this week, we will determine to look at two types of prayer: Breakthrough Prayer and Defining Prayer.

So kick off your shoes (I know in the last session I had you *put on* some shoes!) and let your feet feel the grass below you. Let it tickle your arches and bend between your toes like a lush green carpet that ushers you into the presence of God. I can't wait to spend this next week together frolicking in the *prayer grass* of God.

GROUP DISCUSSION (approx. 25 minutes)

Discuss the following questions based on the week two personal study.

1. Jesus speaks directly to our tendency to make prayer a formula. The NIV quotes him saying, "When you pray, do not keep on babbling," while the NASB uses these words: "When you are praying, do not use meaningless repetition." Have you ever felt like you babbled in prayer, repeating yourself in meaningless repetition with no real heart connection to God? If possible, give an example.

2. What do you think Jesus meant when he said, "The spirit is willing but the flesh is weak," regarding our feeble attempts to pray?

3. Do you sometimes mistake worry for prayer? How are they different?

4. In the seeking phase of prayer, there are many things we aren't sure of — but fortunately, we can count on a few things: God is a God of redemption (2 Peter 3:9); we can be free (John 8:32); we can have peace (John 14:27); and we don't have to be afraid (Psalm 145:18 – 19). If you find yourself in this seeking phase of prayer, share which of these assurances is most needed in your life now.

5. If grit means determination, fortitude, perseverance, and bravery, how is grit essential to prayer?

6. How does the promise that God answers all our prayers (yes, no, and not yet ... but coming soon) clarify the fact that you *are* being heard when you pray?

7. Have you ever cried out to God in a language that mingles praying with crying — *prying*? When was the last time you *pried* in prayer? Does knowing that Jesus was "a man of sorrows, acquainted with grief" reassure you?

8. If you have other insights or questions from last week's personal study, share them now as time permits.

VIDEO TEACHING (22 minutes)

Watch the video. The main points are included here for you. Jot down additional notes if you wish.

We have different prayer moods when we pray.

Breakthrough prayer is the type of praying we do when we can't stand our lives the way they are for one more minute.

Hannah was a woman in Scripture who needed a breakthrough (1 Samuel 1).

- She struggled with infertility and the taunting of a wife who shared her husband.
- She was in the throes of a depression.
- She poured her heart out to God on the steps of the temple.
- The priest Eli thought she was drunk, but she explained she was desperate for a breakthrough with God.

Just when we think we can't take it one more minute, God reveals himself either by the swift shifting of circumstances or the gentle shift of our attitude toward them—either way, it's a breakthrough.

Defining prayer takes place when we answer a searing question that Jesus calmly asks—for instance, "Do you wish to get well?" (John 5:6 NASB).

Why would Jesus ask this, knowing the man had struggled with paralysis for thirty-eight years?

Sometimes we cling to the very things that paralyze us.

Jesus says, "Get up! Pick up your mat and walk." We can't get up and stay stuck in our paralysis at the same time. If we really want to change habits, behaviors, or attitudes, we have to have the clarity of this *defining* type of prayer. To answer "yes" requires that we get up, take what we've been laying on (excuses), and move.

PERSONAL STUDY

DAY ONE BREAKTHROUGH PRAYER

Before I had kids, I found it amusing to watch young moms flail in their verbal tirades as they tried to corral their young into a state of proper behavior. I'll never forget one mom I watched outside an apartment we were renting in Denver. She had ten bags of groceries, four cranky kids, and two flights of stairs to tackle as she tried to reach her apartment. One of her boys was sobbing because she hadn't let him buy the toy he wanted. Another son was teasing the youngest by grabbing her blankie and swinging it over his head like he had just won an Olympic race. The last of the four held on to his mother's leg, each step inching closer to a full dragging of his body weight by her toned calf muscle. As the mom neared the base of the stairs, she belted out a sentence that held the power of a jackhammer as it pierced the moans and whines of their poor behavior. "That's it! Not one more minute of this ... not one more minute!"

I quickly rushed to her side and asked what I could do to help. Grabbing bags of groceries, I knew she was at a breaking point and her kids knew it too; suddenly they became well-behaved cherubs, marching in a row behind her like little ducks on the shore of a pond.

This mom had a moment of clarity (either that or a mental breakdown!). She reached a point of no return. She simply couldn't take it anymore and had to cry out. This is the core of Breakthrough Prayer. It's the type of praying we do when we can't stand our lives the way they are for another minute. Nothing short of a breakthrough will do.

There's a woman in Scripture who had to have a breakthrough. As a matter of fact, her breakthrough left her life and the lives of her family profoundly altered. This woman's name was Hannah.

Hannah lived at a time when she had to share her husband with another wife. For the life of me, I can't figure out why anyone ever thought that was manageable, but that's the condition she lived with. To make matters worse, this "rival" wife had a quiver full of children, while Hannah had none. Year after year Hannah prayed, and remained barren for such a long period that the taunting and teasing of this rival wife became unbearable.

Please turn to 1 Samuel 1 and read verses 1–7. How did Peninnah treat Hannah and what was Hannah's response (vv. 6–7)?

Have you ever endured harsh treatment to the point that you couldn't take it anymore? Something inside you snapped, and you had to express your discomfort in some way. What does "snapping" look like for you?

Hannah was at a breaking point, her depressed behavior evident. What does her husband say to her in verse 8 that indicates the depth of her despair?

Hannah was about to take a breakdown and turn it into a breakthrough. What did she do in verses 9–11?

It's interesting to note that Hannah didn't care what it looked like; she went to the temple stairs and began to wail before God. I love this woman. I'm an extreme fan of people who are real before God. As she prayed, she laid out some specific points for God to consider.

What were some of the things she asked God for, and what did she offer him in prayer (v. 11)?

It's clear that Hannah was a woman familiar with praying. She had probably lifted this petition to God on countless occasions, but this day was different. She needed a breakthrough, and I don't think she could have been pried off the temple stairs without one.

What did Eli say to Hannah as he watched her pray (vv. 12–14)?

Eli was a recognized priest in Shiloh. But sadly, he was perhaps most known for the poor behavior of his own sons, Hophni and Phinehas. Little did he realize how profoundly Hannah's prayer was going to one day affect his own life. It's possible that Eli had been caught up in the routine business of serving God for so long that he didn't recognize someone truly engaging God in prayer.

What was Hannah's response to him in verse 15? Please write it out below.

Whether Eli was truly touched or whether he was just trying to get this emotional woman off the steps of his temple, we'll never know. But he did offer Hannah words that seemed to confirm the release she was feeling in her formerly troubled spirit.

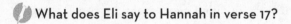 **What does Eli say to Hannah in verse 17?**

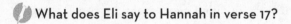 **Now here's the remarkable thing about a breakthrough. Look at verse 18 and describe how Hannah left the steps of the temple after praying.**

At this point, she wasn't pregnant. She had no idea that one day she would give birth to one of the most beloved prophets in Israel — but she left that place transformed. Whether God chooses to change a circumstance, or whether he changes *us in* the circumstance … either way, it's a breakthrough.

Let's examine the process of a breakthrough to see if your life needs a prayer makeover in this area.

1. *I am afflicted.* Is there an area of your life that has plagued you to the point of feeling you can't take it for one more minute?

2. *Remember me, Lord; don't forget me as I cry out my request!* Recall your love for the Lord, and remind him of your love and commitment to him. This isn't about what you can get from him, but rather about your love for him.

3. *I will have a role in this commitment.* For Hannah, this meant a promise to deliver the child she prayed for into the Lord's service. Her prayer came with a caveat that she would participate in the outcome of God's favor. She would bless him with the gift in which he blessed her. Is the prayer of your breakthrough laced with a commitment that centers on blessing God?

4. *I don't care who is watching.* Often when we pray for breakthroughs, people around us (including those who love us) don't understand. They may think you're taking things too far, or should simply resign yourself to the fact that things will never

change. Do you need to model Hannah and pray regardless of what people think?

5. *I am no longer sad. I have release.* When Hannah left the temple, she was different, even though her circumstances weren't … yet! She knew God had listened, and she believed that things were going to change. Is God stirring you toward a release in prayer? A point where you know he is moving?

It's important to note that we're not talking about a soda machine relationship with God here. The type you put in the change and out pops what you want. We're talking about a maturity that respects God's authority and penmanship over our lives, yet desires a mutual level of trust so gutsy that we're sure our lives will never be the same. Jim Cymbala describes this place of intimacy when he writes:

> The Spirit of God is able to grant a profound inner assurance that what we have asked for has been granted. Some earlier Christians used the term "praying through" to describe the supplication that stays at the throne of grace until this assurance has been granted. Rather than the human-centered "name it and claim it" formula, this is the "pray it and know it" cycle that comes from the Holy Spirit.[11]

If you find yourself in need of a breakthrough today, don't let another minute pass by without climbing onto the steps of God's temple (kneeling on the floor of your family room, crying out beside the piles of laundry, lying across your bed) and entreating him for it. Write your prayer to God here.

Often, after I read certain authors who explain concepts like this to me I'm left feeling inspired, but a little frustrated. I want to ask them, "What have you really endured in your life? Have you ever felt pain that has ripped your insides into a thousand pieces?" For me, only an author who can answer yes to this question is someone I can trust.

It's easy to preach to people about a breakthrough when your life has never been broken. I can assure you, sweet sister, my life has been broken more times than I can count. I have crawled up on my steps before God and begged him to break through my fog, and often, my attitude toward the fog. So, like friends grasped arm in arm, let's pray for our breakthroughs—and wait in hushed wonder to see how they are delivered.

GOING DEEPER (OPTIONAL)

I mentioned in today's personal study that the priest Eli's life would be profoundly changed by the gutsy prayer Hannah moaned on the stairs of his temple. Although Eli was not an effective father, he was a faithful mentor to Hannah's son Samuel. Look at a few scenes that took place after Hannah's breakthrough:

- The birth and deliverance of her son to God's service: 1 Samuel 1:19 – 28
- Samuel's childhood and the blessings bestowed on Hannah's faithfulness: 1 Samuel 2:18 – 21
- The prophetic call of Samuel: 1 Samuel 3:1 – 21

After reading these passages, are you left with a sense of God's purpose? When you think about it, so many lives were touched by Hannah's breakthrough: her husband Elkanah, the mean wife Peninnah, Samuel's younger brothers and sisters, the priest Eli, his awful sons, and eventually all of Israel. Breakthroughs aren't meant just for the one praying; they're meant to bring refreshment and wonder to all those stroked by the hand of God as they watch a breakthrough unfold.

DAY TWO BREAKING THROUGH TOGETHER

> Two are better than one, because they have a good return for their labor: if either of them falls down, one can help the other up. But pity anyone who falls, and has no one to help them up. (Ecclesiastes 4:9–10)

The first time I read these verses, I was stunned. I spent years as a child and young adult living like a lone ranger. I had lots of friends, and was even deemed popular, but few really knew me. That was too risky. Truthfully, I didn't even know myself. When I came to understand the love of Jesus at age twenty, I threw myself into his arms with the fervor of a lost child running toward weeping parents. In the safety of those arms, I learned what it meant to trust people. To let them into my life without the fear that I may let them down, or worse, lose them.

If you have friends in your life who surround you with love and encouragement, consider yourself blessed; but if you feel lonely, fake, or forgotten—remember the words God spoke through the writer of Ecclesiastes: you only need one other person to help you when you fall.

I once heard a man say, "If we come to the end of our lives with one person who truly knows and loves us, our lives have been rich." It may be a sister, husband, child, neighbor, parent, or friend who holds you when you fall, but the simplicity of the Scripture is this: we need someone's hands to help us when we fall, and with two hands we see far better return on whatever we set our minds to.

This is never more evident than with prayer. Jesus says, *"If two of you on earth agree about anything they ask for, it will be done for them by my Father in heaven. For where two or three gather in my name, there I am with them"* (Matthew 18:19–20).

Notice he doesn't say when you're in a crowd, or in a stadium filled with people; he simply says two or three. He's not saying crowds are bad, or that he's not present in those types of settings. He's simply explaining the power of two people joining their hearts in prayer.

There's a story in the Bible that makes me laugh every time I read it. It's the story of people gathering to pray, and the giddy confusion they experienced when they realized God heard their cry for a breakthrough. This anxious group gathered in the house of Mary, the mother of Mark, to pray for the apostle Peter, who had been abruptly arrested and taken from their midst.

I picture them huddled up, two or three to a group, lifting their cries to God for Peter's safety. Maybe there was a leader who helped them voice their prayers collectively, or maybe you could hear the muffled sound of everyone praying to themselves, weeping entangled with petition, as they asked a miraculous favor from the God they loved.

Please turn to Acts 12 and read verses 1–4. Who did Herod kill and what was the reaction of the Jews toward the killing?

This lust for bloodshed led to the seizing of Peter. It's important to understand that Peter was the leader of the early church. He was their trusted pastor, the person whom everyone looked to for guidance—he was the one who slept, ate, and walked with Jesus. To say the church was devastated is an understatement. They knew what Herod had done to James and begged God to mercifully save Peter from this same fate. If ever someone needed a breakthrough, it was Peter.

Write verse 5 below. What was the church fervently doing on Peter's behalf?

Please read verses 6–19 and put the following events in the order (1–5) in which they occurred.

_____ Peter continued to knock, and when they saw him they were amazed.

_____ An angel of the Lord suddenly appeared and a light shone in the cell; he struck Peter's side and said, "Get up quickly." And the chains fell off Peter's hands.

_____ Peter went to the house of Mary, the mother of John, where many were gathered together to pray.

_____ Peter followed the angel, but couldn't figure out if what was happening was real, or if he was seeing a vision.

_____ Rhoda heard a knock at the door of the gate and went to answer it, but when she heard Peter's voice she was so excited she ran to tell the others and forgot to open the gate!

It must have been a rowdy prayer gathering once Peter showed up. After poor Rhoda laughed her head off at herself, I imagine they all stuck to Peter like burrs on a boot. There's something about praying for a breakthrough with someone else that makes it all the more emotional when you see it transpire.

For ten years I had a group of friends who gathered to pray. We called ourselves the _Upper Room Prayer Girls_ because we met in my upstairs bedroom—draped over the bed, on the floor, or on chairs. We were a lively bunch that loved God and loved each other. The funny thing about that group is you never knew who might show up. Once a ninety-year-old woman graced our gathering, brought by one of the regular attendees; she offered stories of wisdom and prayer that could knock your socks off. We had an open-door policy where people could come and go as they liked, but one thing was for sure: it always felt like we just had a spiritual massage. We prayed for everything in that group: fears, struggling relationships, health concerns, job desires, financial needs, spiritual insight, hopes and dreams of doing great things for God. Sometimes we worked the kinks out of our prayer muscles and sometimes we just rested in the relaxing rub of the Holy Spirit's caress.

I could share hundreds of stories of breakthroughs we witnessed in that group, but one stands out. It's the story of my dear friend Jen and her husband, John. Jen and I taught school together, and prayed for many breakthroughs in her life. We prayed for her sick mama before she passed away; we prayed for the birth of her two sons after years of infertility. But then something transpired that shook her to the core and tore at the threads of her family's fabric. This life-changing jolt was the bipolar struggles of her beloved John.

The mental illness—high-climaxing mania and crushingly low depression—seemed to come on suddenly, although Jen may have missed earlier signs. Year after year we prayed for healing as John spiraled into dangerous behavior that once left him in a strange city, unable to make his way home. Jen dreaded holidays, as even putting up a Christmas tree felt too challenging for her bedridden husband.

Aided by a maze of doctors, medicine, books, and wisdom from others, Jen navigated her way through these murky waters. As bad as she felt, John felt worse. Typically a loving Christian husband and father, he was shattered by the helpless state he found himself in, unable to see his way out of the funnel cloud that hovered over his life.

We prayed winters, springs, summers, and falls—never giving up hope for a breakthrough in his cycles of distress. Over time, I watched Jen change. Her patience, which was always evident, was now outstanding. She would leave John love notes and Scriptures of assurance. Sometimes she felt like running from the pain and loss of normalcy, but instead she dug in and loved.

Then, one day everything changed. Bedridden again from the dark pull of depression, John suddenly got up, showered, and drove to meet Jen as she helped her sister move into a new apartment. He stood by his car, tears streaming down his face, and explained he'd had a breakthrough. The whole family gathered around him to pray, and that Sunday at church he stood up in the midst of a large congregation proclaiming that his life had been touched. The darkness had been defeated. And although John continues to faithfully take the medicine the doctors recommend, he knows his healing is an answer to many, many prayers.

The gift of praying for breakthroughs with another person is an honor that can't be measured in words—it can only be measured by hope and the tender assurance to stand by someone who needs to be lifted after a fall. Two are better than one, and when two gather, Jesus listens. May we find fellow gatherers to lift us, and may we be lifters of those who feel that no one cares when they've fallen.

GOING DEEPER (OPTIONAL)

Paul was a man devoted to praying for others. When he uttered commands such as, "Pray without ceasing" (1 Thessalonians 5:17 NASB), he not only gave an invitation for us to follow, but he modeled it in his own life.

I've recently taken a few sentences he wrote to the people in Colossae and put them on an index card so I can cover people God brings to mind with these words. They're also packed with power if you want to pray them with someone else. Enjoy his words below:

> For this reason, since the day we heard about you, we have not stopped praying for you. We continually ask God to fill you with the knowledge of his will through all the wisdom and understanding that the Spirit gives, so that you may live a life worthy of the Lord and please him in every way: bearing fruit in every good work, growing in the knowledge of God, being strengthened with all power according to his glorious might so that you might have great endurance and patience, and giving joyful thanks to the Father, who has qualified you to share in the inheritance of his holy people in the kingdom of light. (Colossians 1:9 – 12)

What a gloriously long run-on sentence! Write this sentence in your journal and pray chunks of it over your own life, and the lives of the people you love throughout the week.

DAY THREE DEFINING PRAYER

No part of my Bible has been traveled like the fifth chapter of John. If I were sitting beside you (which I wish I were), you would see a long piece of yellowed tape holding the page together—similar to the way this chapter has held together my life.

John 5 is the story of a paralyzed man. He's not only physically paralyzed, but emotionally attached to the very things that paralyze him.

Please turn to John 5 and read verses 1–9. How long had this man been lying in his condition?

What did Jesus ask him in verse 6? Please write it out below.

The fact that Jesus saw him and *knew* he'd been in that condition a long time speaks volumes. You'd think he would walk up to the man, feel pity for him, and heal him—no questions asked. But instead Jesus asked one of the most important questions in Bible: "Do you want to get well?"

Why ask a paralyzed man if he wants to get well? As crazy as it sounds, sometimes the answer to that poignant question is, "No."

Have you ever prayed for something intensely, but then squirmed at the thought of doing what it takes to be free? I speak to countless women who hate their bodies or struggle with health issues due to their weight, but when presented with a plan to "get well," choose to keep praying instead of moving or changing.

Often the paralysis may look like a wound inflicted on your life: divorce, abuse, betrayal, indifference. After years of praying for the wound to heal, when Jesus offers a path of forgiveness and new skin to cover old scar tissue, we choose bitterness over new life.

I fought the "Do you want to get well?" question with the force of a grenade, ready to explode at anyone who doubted my motives. My combat zone was food. How can anything as normal as eating turn to war? Just ask someone who goes on countless diets, loses the same five to thirty pounds over and over again, and binges, purges, or starves herself into submission.

After years of struggle, I finally decided to do something about it. I studied diet and health books like I was studying for the bar exam. With a newfound knowledge and determination, I began to lose weight, and boy, did it feel good. It felt so good that I couldn't stop. Each five pounds that I shed brought new elation. I won the battle. I was a new me.

The trouble was, when my body began to protectively put a few pounds back on, unable to sustain itself at the weight I pushed to maintain, I completely lost it. The war without was now the war within. Ultimately, my battle wasn't so much with food as it was with insecurity and control. When Jesus asked me, "Do you want to get well?" I really didn't know how to respond. I knew I didn't want to die — and I was on a fast track to that very destination if I didn't stop fighting — but I was used to my rituals and routines and feeling in control.

Responding to Jesus' question came in waves for me. There was the initial "Yes, I want to get well," followed by, "What do I have to do to get there?"

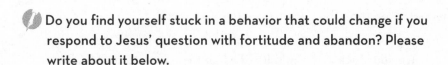 **Do you find yourself stuck in a behavior that could change if you respond to Jesus' question with fortitude and abandon? Please write about it below.**

After Jesus asked the question, the paralyzed man instantly protested. What excuse did he offer Jesus in verse 7?

I could kick myself for the time I've wasted blaming my behavior on somebody else. We could fill a book with excuses as to why we've ended up where we are, and some excuses are truly valid, but what about why we *stay stuck* there? That's the real intent of Jesus' question. He knows what's gotten us there, but asks if we want out.

While *Breakthrough Prayer* opens new doorways to walk through, *Defining Prayer* mobilizes the steps we take to walk through them. Defining Prayer takes good intent and turns it to changed behavior.

List the three things Jesus told this man to do in verse 8.

The first thing Jesus instructs is simply, "Get up," yet this is often anything but simple. Being the daughter of a paralyzed man, I know what those legs looked like. They were thin strips of flesh hung loosely on brittle bones, nowhere near ready for walking. Yet Jesus says to stand up on those legs, even if we think we can't.

Are you stuck in the middle of a habit you long to change, but don't think you can? Are there parts of your life that you've silently put into the "never will change" category? Are you so overwhelmed with where to begin, that staying stuck seems more appealing? Please explain.

If you answered yes to any of these questions you're in good company. Anyone who has ever really committed to change in their lives has to face these questions head on. When Jesus told the man to get up, instantly our friend at the pool had to decide whether to stand or keeping lying on his mat. You can't do both.

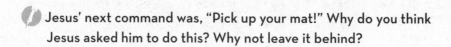 Jesus' next command was, "Pick up your mat!" Why do you think Jesus asked him to do this? Why not leave it behind?

I believe Jesus told the man to roll up his mat and take it with him so that he would never forget what Jesus had saved him from. When we tuck "old mats" under our arms and move, it gives us the credibility to tell others, "I used to be paralyzed by _____, but now I'm different, and you can be different too."

Finally, Jesus commanded the man to walk. Notice he didn't start there. The man first had to get up, take what he'd been lying on (excuses, habits, old beliefs), and then move.

Friend, if you and I are willing to get up and move, Jesus will transform us. From crawling to running, from hiding to basking in his glory, from lying on a filthy mat to tucking it under our arms and moving on. Today, if you or someone you love needs to answer the defining "Do you want to get well?" question, please don't run from it. I wasted years lying on my mat, afraid of walking because I was used to being paralyzed. Answer "yes" to Jesus' question even if you don't know how your legs will work. He simply wants you to get up, and he will strengthen you to take each step with the new legs he gives you. Suddenly, a dirty mat doesn't look so appealing!

GOING DEEPER (OPTIONAL)

One of the things I love about God is he continues to nudge areas of our lives that need to change. He doesn't barge his way into these areas; he reveals them to us, and then waits to be invited in. When Jesus healed the paralyzed man, he first asked a question that had a defining effect on the way the man lived the rest of his life. His questions have a way of exposing our motives, beliefs, habits, and attitudes.

My mom is one of the bravest people I know. After my father's car accident, she fought a fierce battle with alcoholism that spanned a decade. After several attempts to quit drinking, the reality of her helplessness and surrender became evident. She entered AA and fully committed her life to getting well, and has been completely sober for more than thirty years. Not a day goes by that I don't thank him for his redeeming grace and redefinition.

For anyone who's ever thought they were a hopeless case, that their problems are uglier than other people's, that God can't change them because they're too messed up—please understand that Jesus asks, "Do you want to get well?" with the sweetest look of compassion and encouragement. He's not using a voice of belittling condemnation, but inviting us to an assurance of wild grace.

Take a few moments to write a defining prayer to God in your journal. How do you respond to Jesus' question, and how will you let him *redefine* who you are?

DAY FOUR DEFINING BEAUTY

Yesterday I treated myself to a pedicure. There's nothing like having your feet rubbed, scraped, and prettied. The trouble is I have awful toenails. Because I'm a runner (don't be too impressed; my motto is, "As slow as you can go"), sometimes an entire toenail has fallen off right in the pedicurist's hands! They look at me with disdain as I simply mutter, "It's okay; something else will grow in its place." I've never claimed to be glamorous, but I do admit my desire to be!

As I sat in the nail salon chair skimming pictures in a women's magazine, my eyes went straight for the pictures of beautiful faces, gorgeous hair, stunning clothes, and flawless skin. Who can measure up to the standard these women have set for glamour in our society?

Of course, in church circles, the spiritual thing to say is we don't care what we look like. It's not important to God, so it shouldn't be important to us. But often how we look on the outside is a reflection of how we feel on the inside. Do we look plastic, disheveled, overdone, messy, disheartened, flamboyant, tidy, or pulled together? Truthfully, I've never known one single woman who doesn't care, even a little, about being attractive. I think it's wired in our DNA from Eve.

The tricky part is how to define attractiveness. What qualifies as attractive to God? Sarah, Abraham's wife was described as physically beautiful. She was so stunning that Abraham lied twice about her being his sister instead of his wife, so he wouldn't be killed (Genesis 12:13; 20:2)! Esther went through months of spa treatment before being presented to the king (Esther 2:12–13), and was initially chosen solely for her good looks. So where does this leave us? Is it wrong to want to be attractive? And more important, how does God define beauty?

The book of Proverbs contains many flowing descriptions of women from God's perspective. Chapter after chapter outlines what he loves in a woman, and what he hates.

 Please turn to Proverbs 7 and read verses 6–27. How does the writer, likely Solomon, describe this woman in verse 11?

✦ **Verse 19 indicates that she's married, but she doesn't care. What does she have her mind set on (vv. 16–18)?**

✦ **How does God describe her fate in verses 26–27?**

I have a special disdain for this woman, because she's made her way into my marriage. Maybe you've encountered this woman too. Seductive, beautiful, flirty, coy—like a groupie waiting for a movie star, she doesn't care who else loves this man; she wants him. Not to adore him, or share her true beauty with him, but to destroy him. Such dangerous beauty is ugly to God. It's marred and disfigured, because though this woman may be physically attractive, her spirit is rotting with lies and deceit.

✦ **Now turn to Proverbs 14 and write verse 1 below.**

This woman has a beauty that's distinguished by her wisdom. A wise woman builds her home, while a foolish one tears it down. I've often pondered how we can tear down the things that mean the most to us. I know for me it's looked like nagging, pushing, and controlling. But gradually I've learned to focus most of my attention on the building part of this verse: praying, encouraging, walking alongside, listening, hoping, and helping.

✦ **What does *building* your home look like?**

It's fitting that Solomon ends the book of Proverbs with one of the most detailed descriptions of beauty. I used to roll my eyes when I read this passage, just like I roll my eyes when I see unattainable beauty in the pages of a magazine. But I've made peace with this woman. Actually, I think I've become this woman as God has pruned and purged my model of beauty and replaced it with his.

Please read Proverbs 31:10 – 31. What is this woman's attitude toward her husband, and how does he feel about her (vv. 10 – 12)?

Verses 13 – 16 explain her business sense and creative ability to help her family thrive. I see women every day who do this effectively: teachers and maids, moms and executives.

How do you contribute to the way your family survives? If you're single, how do you sustain yourself?

Verses 17 – 19 illustrate that this woman isn't lazy! She's on the move, and she knows that what she's doing is good.

Do you have purpose and assurance as a woman? If not, what do you think is causing you to feel lack of purpose?

What do you notice about our girl in verse 20, and how is this quality a form of beauty?

Jot down words in verses 25–28 that remind you of how you want to be described by God.

The final description of this woman slams a home run in God's favor. It's the description we've been waiting for, and it's worth the wait. Please write out verse 30 below.

It doesn't get simpler than that. God says, *"Charm is deceptive and beauty is fleeting, but a woman who fears the LORD is to be praised."* Beauty isn't the problem; it's okay but fleeting—but honoring God will bring lasting praise. It's our love for him that stands out and is ultimately seen as beautiful.

I feel a sense of wonder as I realize that God's beauty, God's scent, the fragrance of Christ is what lingers long after we've left a room. People won't remember how good your hair looked, or how well you zipped your jeans … but they will remember the look of love your eyes splashed over theirs. I only wish we saw *that* kind of beauty in magazines.

DAY FIVE BEFORES AND AFTERS

Yesterday I shared how I peruse magazines glancing at pictures that show cute hair, clothes, a kitchen makeover, or shabby chic decorating. But my favorite part of any fashion or home magazine is the *before* and *after* pictures. I love looking at a *before*—riddled with imperfection or unflattering styles and colors—and seeing it transform into an *after*. I find myself gasping at the radical difference even small changes can make. A different twist of bangs or a color change in makeup; a couch moved from the back of the room to the center; a vase of flowers placed in just the right spot—can swap a boring *before* into an intriguing *after*.

The same can be said for our lives. If you could peek at my *before* photo, here's what you'd see: insecure, scared, worried, picking at scars, impatient, selfish, always trying the new cure for wandering (diet, skin product, money making pursuit, exercise craze), mildly interested in God but nothing too radical, critical, lonely. Thankfully, my *befores* are being transformed into *afters*, thanks to the brilliant hand of a God who specializes in makeovers.

Today I'd like us to look at three women in Scripture who had radical *befores* and *afters*. Two of these ladies were stuck in a society that fueled their poor choices; the other woman was stuck in a body she couldn't stand.

Please turn to John 8 and read verses 1–11. Because we may be familiar with this story, it's tempting to brush it off like old news, but there's so much about this woman we don't know.

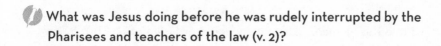 **What was Jesus doing before he was rudely interrupted by the Pharisees and teachers of the law (v. 2)?**

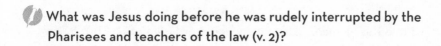 **How do the accusers describe the woman they brought to him (v. 4)?**

Some interesting questions arise from this scene:

- The woman was caught "in the act," but where was the man, who was also subject to stoning?
- Where would a person go to catch someone in this act? How would the Pharisees, noted for their claim to holiness, have known where to go?
- While the Mosaic law prescribed stoning for adultery, this penalty was not imposed in the first century. Rabbinic courts rigorously avoided imposing it, so why would the Pharisees throw it in Jesus' face as they did?[12]

The Pharisees couldn't have cared less about this woman; they just wanted to make Jesus look bad. But Jesus couldn't have cared more for the woman; he just wanted to set her free.

Some authors believe that when Jesus stooped to the ground to write, he was writing the Ten Commandments; others believe he may have been listing out the sins of those men who pulled this woman—barely clothed or naked—in front of a crowd to humiliate her. Whatever the case, Jesus was about to gracefully turn a *before* into an *after*.

 What did Jesus say to this woman in verses 10 and 11? Please write his words below.

Jesus told this woman, *"Go now and leave your life of sin,"* but many women stuck in the web of prostitution were there because of a society that offered meager ways for women to support themselves. For some, it was a grim necessity. They would have been as much victims as victimizers.[13]

Jesus didn't condemn the woman, but he also didn't condone her behavior. He told her to change. Her life could no longer sustain the sin since it had been touched by the Savior.

My all-time favorite book is *Redeeming Love*, a novel by Francine Rivers. In it, Francine describes the life of a woman named Angel, who watches her mother practice a brand of upscale prostitution. Later, as a hungry, scared young woman with nowhere else to turn, Angel is forced into the life she cursed as a youth. It takes the love of a godly man, and the love of a Savior she doesn't yet know, to coax her out of the web of lies that whispers the only worth she has is the body she can sell.

I've never sold my body, but I've punished and abused it on many occasions. I've heard the despicable lie that tells me I'm not worth anything and that I don't matter.

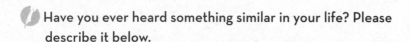 **Have you ever heard something similar in your life? Please describe it below.**

I wish we could see this woman in the weeks and years following her encounter with Jesus. My fondest hope is that she let her *before* become an *after* ... for good.

The next woman we'll study struggled with something that wasn't her choice. Her body turned on her and became her adversary. Turn to Luke 13 and read verses 10 – 17.

How did Luke, a trained physician, describe this woman in verse 11?

It's interesting that the minute Jesus saw her, he called to her. She had probably attended this synagogue for nearly two decades, but I wonder if anyone had really "seen" her before.

Have you ever felt invisible, that others didn't see you despite your presence in the room (perhaps even in the church sanctuary)? What was that like?

What was this woman's reaction after Jesus straightened her spine (v. 13)?

Eighteen years is a long time to live with your eyes to the ground. You'd think everyone would have been jumping and dancing with this woman, but they weren't. What was the synagogue ruler's reaction to this miracle, and how did Jesus respond to his criticism (vv. 14–16)?

In their book *Every Woman in the Bible*, Sue and Larry Richards contrast the differences between this ruler and the bent woman.[14] See if anything strikes you.

	The Ruler	The Woman
Status	Spiritual leader	Member of the congregation
Characteristics	Male, authority, healthy	Female, victim, crippled
Jesus	Rebuked him, condemned him	Restored her, affirmed her
Outcome	Was shamed	Became a cause for rejoicing

What I love most about this woman is that she kept showing up. Week after week, she attended a synagogue in which she was forgotten, until the day that Jesus "saw" her. At the right moment in her history, he straightened her life—and that congregation was never the same.

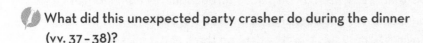 Is your life bent over? Do you need to be seen by Jesus today? Write two to three sentences asking Jesus to touch your life in a way that causes rejoicing not only in you, but in those watching.

The final woman we'll walk with today is well known for her hair. It's not the style or color that was stunning, but what she used it for ... to wipe Jesus' feet with her tears. Turn to Luke 7 and read verses 36–50.

The Pharisee mentioned in this Scripture is a man named Simon. At first glance, you might think he was a great man, having Jesus over for dinner and all. But Simon wanted to entertain Jesus, not worship him. He wanted to be seen *with* him, not be known *by* him. This reminds me of so many today who walk around with crosses around their necks and curses in their mouths. The symbols of Jesus may look good on their hats, shirts, and jewelry, but don't ask them to explain who Jesus is, because frankly, they won't know.

What did this unexpected party crasher do during the dinner (vv. 37–38)?

Have you ever witnessed a scene so emotional that some people in the room made inappropriate remarks because they were uncomfortable? I once witnessed a man emotionally express his love for God and brokenness before him. His wife was so uncomfortable with his sudden expression of love that she kept shushing him. I about shushed her out of my living room!

Here in Luke 7 was a woman known to everyone as a prostitute pouring her love over Jesus with tears. There are some settings you can't sugarcoat, and this was one of them.

What was Simon's inappropriate remark that he uttered only to himself (v. 39)?

Simon came to Jesus out of curiosity and disbelief, while the woman came to Jesus in pursuit of hope and forgiveness. What a difference their postures make.

The woman brought a vial of the most expensive thing she owned, her perfume. Some believe this vial may have cost her a year's pay, but it also symbolized what she put on before she'd go to the men in her old life— smelling of rich bouquets but inwardly reeking of despair.

What does she do with the perfume to mark the end of her old life and the beginning of a new life (v. 38)?

I've often used symbols to mark a transition from old to new. I have rocks that I've written on displayed throughout my home to mark a "monument" or time that God has shown me a new way of thinking or believing. Sometimes I write a date on them and a phrase to remind me of the reason I want to remember. After Joshua led the Israelites across the Jordan River into the Promised Land, he asked them to pick up twelve stones so they could build a memorial. The purpose of the memorial was so they could look at the stones and remember what God had done for them. I wonder if the empty alabaster vial of perfume would now be this woman's monument, set somewhere obvious in her home so she could remember.

What did Jesus say to the woman in verse 50 that indicates a personal miracle has taken place? Write his words below.

Friend, our faith saves us and we go in peace. This faith is utterly stunned that Jesus can take the shameful fragments of our lives and fill them with purpose. It understands that he sees us and straightens our bent bodies and minds, and it wraps itself in the knowledge that no sin is too big for him to forgive.

Yesterday I shared that my marriage had been marred by the kind of woman that we just studied. I woke this morning thinking about that kind of woman, and wonder if anyone reading this has *been* that woman. As I walked around a quiet lake praying before sunrise, I thought about what I would say to her now that I've had years of healing to wear as a protective cloak around that tender part of my heart. I want to offer the same words that Jesus did: "Go now and leave your life of sin. Your faith has saved you; go in peace."

These words have untwisted the mangled limbs of my life more times than I can count. May they untwist anyone who is willing to look the Savior in the eyes and change their *before* into an *after*.

Session

Four

The GUTS
to BELIEVE

I have a shirt that smells. It's been washed, worn, and slept in for over twenty-one years. For the life of me, I can't bear to think of going to bed in anything but this shirt. It's a T-shirt that Bobby wore for batting practice when he played for the Kansas City Royals. Our son, Colton, was six months old then; this year he graduates from college—and I feel like I'm just getting this shirt broken in.

I'm coziest in my Royals shirt, but often not performing my best in it. Let's put it this way, if I ran into you while wearing this shirt, you would probably get into your car murmuring, "Wow, Gari's really let herself go!" Unfortunately, what's most comfortable isn't always what's going to help us grow spiritually. Often I choose comfy "Royals" faith over gutsy belief. When it comes to faith, we have to get out of our T-shirts (bathrobes, sweatshirts, baggy sweatpants) and believe!

We've talked a lot about prayer, but what about believing *after* we've prayed? This can be the hardest part. Do we believe God is big enough to deal with what we've asked for? Do we believe he'll come through with an answer to our cries for direction, relief, insight, change, healing, or hope?

If prayer is a nail, belief is the hammer that pounds it in place. This is the grappling nature of faith. So with hammers in hand, and cozy faith put aside— let's put our belief into place, sweet friends. Let's have the guts to believe.

GROUP DISCUSSION (approx. 25 minutes)

Discuss the following questions based on the week three personal study.

1. Breakthrough prayer comes when we can't stand our lives the way they are for one more minute. Hannah dealt with her need for a breakthrough by praying with surrender and purpose. What might praying with surrender and purpose look like in your own prayer life?

2. Breakthroughs have a process to them. Using Hannah's model, do you see yourself in one of the following areas of process? Explain.

   - I am afflicted.
   - Remember me, Lord; don't forget me as I cry out my request!
   - I will have a role in this commitment.
   - I don't care who is watching.
   - I am no longer sad; I have release.

3. In breakthrough prayer, sometimes God changes circumstances and sometimes he changes *us* in the midst of the circumstance. Why is it important to remember this?

4. How can praying for a breakthrough in a group or even with one other person lighten the load? Surprisingly, many women are uncomfortable praying with others or sharing their innermost needs. How might you come alongside someone like this to offer support and encouragement?

5. Jesus asked a paralyzed man a strange question when he said, *"Do you want to get well?"* (John 5:6). Why wouldn't he want to get well after being confined to a mat for thirty-eight years? Why do you think Jesus asked this question?

6. How do we sometimes cling to the very things — habits, attitudes, bitterness, cycles of destruction passed down generationally — that paralyze us?

7. Have you ever been so overwhelmed with where to begin, that staying stuck seems more appealing? Briefly explain.

8. If we're willing to "get up, take the mat we've been lying on, and move," our lives will be transformed. What might Jesus' command look like in modern circumstances?

9. What characteristics come to mind when you think of a beautiful woman? What comes to mind when you think of *yourself* and the word *beauty*?

10. How does God's description of beauty in Proverbs 31:30 redefine your thinking? If we could see the *before* and *after* pictures of your life, what would we see?

11. If you have other insights or questions from last week's personal study, share them now as time permits.

VIDEO TEACHING (22 minutes)

Watch the video. The main points are included here for you. Jot down additional notes if you wish.

While prayer engages us in conversation with God, belief is the proof we trust the God we pray to. What good does it do to pray, if we don't believe God can change anything we've prayed about?

In order to grow, we need to move out of comfy faith into a gutsy belief in God.

In the gospel of Mark (9:20–24 NASB), a man who brought his seizing boy to Jesus for healing was so overcome with fear that he responded to Jesus' words, *"All things are possible to him who believes,"* with a mess of words that contradicted one another: *"I do believe; help my unbelief!"* This messy part of belief can be called *holy tension.*

Holy tension has some notable characteristics:

Doubt

- A perfect picture of doubt can be seen in Peter when he had the guts to get out of the boat that had been rocked by a storm, and walk to Jesus (Matthew 14:28 – 29).
- When he began to sink he uttered three brilliant words: "Lord, save me!"
- Peter proves that when it comes to belief, doubt isn't the point; getting out of the boat is.

Embarrassment

- Do we feel responsible for God's reputation?
- Embarrassment can rob us of powerful moments.

Spiritual Scar Tissue

- If your life has suffered a wound, scar tissue might cause you to wonder if God is truly good.
- Scar tissue can heal stronger than the tissue was before the wound, allowing for a deeper trust and love for the God who heals.

The seizing boy, touched by Jesus, ironically seemed to get worse, leaving the crowd whispering, "He is dead." Sometimes things we pray for seem dead, but they aren't.

If we ever bump up against these two words in Scripture, take note, because something big is about to happen. The two words are: *"But Jesus ..."*

When we wait for our "But Jesus," nothing will be the same.

PERSONAL STUDY

DAY ONE HOLY TENSION

Today we're going to spend time with a terrified father. His son had seizures so intense he feared his boy would die from them. If you've ever seen someone having a seizure, you know how alarming it is to watch. In my book *Spirit Hunger*, I shared that my husband, Bobby, struggled with seizures for years following an accident in which he was electrocuted. Each time I saw him fall to the ground, I panicked — afraid he wouldn't come back to me when the seizure ran its course. Thankfully, it's been years since Bobby had an episode, and his neurologist eventually took him off all medication. But the other day I encountered a man who wasn't so lucky.

I had gone to the gym for a spin class, where we cycle for miles but never leave the four walls of the room! Our instructor is a big man, muscles like the Hulk bulging from his cutoff T-shirt. He doesn't speak much, but instead barks out commands: "Faster; harder; you can do it!" As I gave him a sweaty look of disdain, I noticed that his head began to turn in a circle, much like an owl stretching to see something behind it. Suddenly, he plunged forward, though his feet were still locked in the turning pedals. In a full-blown seizure, his upper body smashed onto the floor while his lower body stayed stuck to the confines of the bike.

I was nearest to him, and leapt from my bike to cradle his bloody head in my arms. Meanwhile, he shook, foamed, and snarled in the throes of a neurological nightmare. The seizure seemed to last forever as people ran screaming for 911. After one seizure finished, he rolled into another.

By the time the ambulance arrived, he was calm, but I was anything but! I couldn't wait to get to my car and cry. It was a fresh reminder of how our friend in Scripture today must have felt every time he held his flailing boy.

🍃 Please turn to Mark 9 and read verses 17–18. How did this father describe what happened to his son during the seizures?

🍃 What do you think his level of desperation was, considering he may have only heard about Jesus by word of mouth?

🍃 Now read verses 20–22. What did Jesus ask the father in verse 21? Please write it below.

If you've ever seen someone seize, it seems strange that in the midst of this boy rolling, foaming, and lurching, Jesus would bother to ask the dad such a question. If I had been in the crowd watching, I may have shouted, "Talk later … heal the boy now!" Yet Jesus gave the man a chance to describe the pain he had lived with since the boy was a child.

🍃 What did the father say at the end of verse 22 that launched one of the most powerful statements Jesus ever made about belief?

🍃 Jesus proclaimed that all things are possible to the one who believes—but the gutsy part of this story is the authentic way the father describes his disbelief. What does he say in verse 24? Please write it below.

In the same breath this man says he believes, but he doesn't believe. Who can't relate to this messy tangle of faith?

Is there something you've prayed about — something that means the world to you — and you find yourself believing ... but not believing? Write about it below.

I call this the *holy tension* of faith — that internal rub that causes friction because it's pulling in two directions. Yet Jesus doesn't leave the father in his spiritual tug-of-war for long.

What did Jesus do in verses 25 – 26 to take charge of this frantic situation?

Here's where things get even stickier. Verse 26 says that the evil spirit cried out and threw the boy into terrible convulsions, after which the boy looked so much like a corpse that people thought he was dead.

Here's a very personal question; answer it as honestly as you can. Have you ever prayed about something, and the situation seemed to get worse? Describe it below.

Often I'm asked if it's possible for things to get worse after we've prayed about them, and my answer is always, "You bet it is." Many times after praying like crazy for something, it looks like I might have been better off not praying—but I know better. Just because something looks dead doesn't mean it is. I'd like you to circle the first two words of the Scripture below.

"But Jesus took him by the hand and raised him, and he got up." (v. 27 NASB)

You just circled two of the most life-changing words in the Bible. Whenever you see them next to each other, pay attention—because something great is about to happen.

What is your *but Jesus*?

- *But Jesus* delivered her from habits and compulsion.
- *But Jesus* healed her body and her mind.
- *But Jesus* came through with the finances and provision.
- *But Jesus* gave her what her heart desired.

Take a few moments to think about your *but Jesus*. Even if things look worse since you dared to pray, how can you push through the holy tension of belief to a place of assurance and thanksgiving? Explain below.

Together let's look for our *but Jesus* moments throughout the day. Even if we start with, "I do believe; help my unbelief!" let's end with, "All things are possible to him who believes."

GOING DEEPER (OPTIONAL)

If you look back to Mark 9:19, you'll see a verse we skipped in our study today, but I'd like to invite you to take a peek at it now.

These are words you might hear from a worn-out mom or tired teacher, but sound strange coming from Jesus. Yet if we examine some of the experiences Jesus had with his disciples in the surrounding chapters of Luke (another account of this same event), we get a better feel as to why Jesus seemed frustrated. Warren Wiersbe says:

> He had given His apostles authority over Satan, yet they were too weak to cast out a demon (Luke 9:37–45). In feeding the five thousand, Jesus gave them an example of compassion, yet they persisted in manifesting selfishness and lack of love (Luke 9:46–56). He taught clearly what it meant to follow Him, yet the volunteers turned out to be "me first" disciples (Luke 9:57–62). No wonder He was grieved![15]

Take a few minutes to read the above Scriptures from Luke, and then write in your journal about how frustrating it must have been at times to be Jesus.

DAY TWO THE HOLY TENSION OF DOUBT

I can picture myself as a young teen—stringy, long hair and bright silver braces wrapped around my teeth—uttering a phrase that defined my world outlook: "I doubt it!" It didn't matter what I was being told, "I doubt it" was my typical response. What happened to the Pollyanna goodness I could see as a child? It seemed "I doubt it" bullied its way to the front of the line, leaving trust and blind faith in people in the dust.

I'm not the only one who suffered a blow from doubt. It seems our whole country morphed from trusting people to doubting cynics. Who can blame us? Everywhere we look we see lying, selfish motives, and empty words that hold no merit.

Nowhere is this more evident than in the workplace. When I worked as an elementary school teacher, staff meetings could turn into a cold dip in an icy pond the minute we grazed topics that teachers differed on. Whispers, rolling eyes, and the vague breeze of irritation could blow us right out of the library if we weren't careful.

One year, our staff decided to take a close look at what the U.S. Department of State calls the *Sevens Norms of Collaborative Work*. It's a study on how coworkers, with their various ideals and beliefs, can create an environment that enables them to move forward in their work rather than getting stuck on their differences.

Of all seven norms, one is absolutely fundamental. As a matter of fact, without it, the others are meaningless. *Presuming positive intent*. Simply put, this is the assumption that other people are acting from positive and constructive intentions.[16]

I know it's tempting to react to this statement with another "I doubt it!" But truthfully, presuming positive intent has changed the way I interact at work, with my husband, children, friends, and even strangers. I wonder what would happen if we presumed positive intent with God rather than doubting him.

I've thought long and hard about doubt and come to the realization that there are two kinds that splash across the canvas of our faith. There's a *productive doubt* that leads to humble belief, and there's *destructive doubt* that keeps us stuck in negative disbelief.

Destructive doubt can't seem to tear itself from these three presumptions:

1. I'm not sure God is good. If he's so good, why is there so much bad?
2. I'm not sure he cares deeply about the issues in my life.
3. I'm not sure his power supersedes the world I live in.

Destructive doubt rips apart belief before we've even finished saying our prayers.

On the other hand, productive doubt recognizes its desire to believe and pushes forward in a graceful state of awe as it watches disbelief crumble in the face of courage and obedience. If we want to make a difference in the lives of those around us, or want God to make a difference in *our* lives, we can learn from the two people we're going to study today.

There are two heroes in our passage: one a young girl who used her unfortunate circumstances to usher a flood of faith over a drought of doubt; and the other a warrior who dared to humble himself—forsaking doubt and clinging to hope.

Please turn to 2 Kings 5 and read this chapter.

Naaman was the captain of the army of the king of Aram. The Arameans ironically had just raided Israel, and in the process had whisked away many captives, among them the young girl in this story.

 How do verses 1–2 describe Naaman and the young girl? Write the description beside each name.

Naaman: _____

Young girl: _____

Our little hero isn't even called by name, but we know that she waited on Naaman's wife with love and care. She was a prisoner, taken from her home and country to serve a man afflicted with leprosy. In Israel, this man would have been shunned from society, but in Aram, he was allowed to climb the ranks of military might. He must have been one brave soldier to be called "valiant" despite the fact that lepers often had missing limbs.

This girl didn't sit quietly or bitterly in her service—she remembered a man of faith in her homeland who believed in a great God (the prophet Elisha), and she told her mistress about him, with the hope that Naaman might receive healing from the God she trusted.

Write what the girl said to her mistress in verse 3 below.

Either she was sweetly convincing, or Naaman was wildly desperate. I think it was a mixture of both. So, with fresh abandon, he went straight to the king of Aram to ask for permission to chase his newfound hope.

What was the king of Israel's response to the king of Aram's letter of request in verse 7?

Israel's king worried that this was political suicide. He certainly had no power to cure this man of leprosy, but how could he say no to a powerful people who had recently pillaged his country? It was a tricky spot. Thank goodness Elisha got wind of the letter.

What did Elisha tell Naaman to do (v. 10) and how did Naaman react to Elisha's directive (vv. 11–12)?

How often we miss something God is trying to do because we let doubt and pride have their way! I remember when I started to write, with the hopes of a career in publishing. I thought I'd quickly be discovered and have my name on a book within a few years. A few years turned into a few decades, as I wrote for any publication that would give me a byline and a cup of coffee. Along the way, I learned that pride and trust can't stand each other. They always end up in a catfight that turns ugly.

 Is there a pocket of pride that may be keeping you from a blessing from God? Ask the Holy Spirit to scour the crevices of your heart on this one. Pride is good at camouflage.

After a large piece of humble pie, Naaman did as Elisha directed. With his skin at last restored to normal, he saw the true God of restoration for the very first time. And imagine the servant girl's reaction when he returned to Aram. She had no idea how her faith and positive outlook would change the life of her master. I think if this young girl could speak to us today, she'd have simple but powerful words to teach us.

- **If you want to make a big difference, be confident.** Her master listened to her because she believed in what she was saying. We have a great God, and there is nothing he can't do. Let's live like we believe it!
- **If you want to make a big difference, be credible.** If her daily service to her mistress hadn't been pleasing, she never would have been taken seriously. People always pay more attention to how we live than to what we say.
- **If you want to make a big difference, speak to people's needs.** Everyone needs hope and help — even powerful or successful people. If the people we desire to help are low on faith, we can lend them some of ours.

- **If you want to make a big difference, don't be afraid to do something even if it seems small.** Some of the most insignificant things we do have the greatest impact.[17]

Even in the holy tension of doubt, we can make a difference if we choose to believe. Faith trumps doubt. As my husband says to the ballplayers he coaches, "It's a no-brainer!"

GOING DEEPER (OPTIONAL)

I wonder what Jesus thinks about doubt. Do you think he gets mad at us when we struggle to believe? I've asked him this question countless times and keep coming back to an incident that occurred after he rose from the grave, but hadn't yet ascended.

Jesus appeared to many of his followers, but one disciple wasn't present at that first appearance. His name was Thomas. Turn to John 20 and read verses 19–29.

In verse 25, Thomas honestly and emphatically announced, *"I will not believe!"* Unless he could see Jesus with his own eyes, he vowed to stay stuck in doubt.

Verse 29 is one that I often say to myself when it comes to belief. Write it in your prayer journal and reflect on what Jesus might say to you about *your* belief.

Sadly, to this day, whenever someone mentions Thomas, he's referred to as "the doubting one." I don't want that nickname—do you?

DAY THREE THE HOLY TENSION OF FEAR

Fear is a force to be reckoned with. I've seen it take women down faster than a linebacker hungry for a tackle. There we are flat on our backs, legs in the air, stunned looks on our faces — as we realize we've been bowled over by a growling opponent. In my opinion, fear is to women what anger is to men. It's our default posture when faith is on vacation.

When my son entered high school, I found myself struggling with fear. This was a topic about which I did plenty of teaching, but now I had to pour myself a heaping spoonful of my own medicine to calm my anxious heart and racing mind. The catalyst for this fear was football.

I'm surrounded by sports. My husband's been in professional baseball for over thirty years; my son-in-law plays professional basketball. But high school football had me in a tight knot. Every Friday I prayed my way through the day as I imagined my skinny son facing giant opponents at the game that night. The problem was Colton was good at football. He made varsity as a sophomore, and never left the field because he held positions on both offense and defense. To top it off, he even returned punts. I'm certain I was the only mother in the stands who yelled, "Lie down! Run out of bounds!" every time he caught a punt or a pass.

Growing up with a quadriplegic father left my imagination plenty of room to run. I pictured Colton's neck snapping after a hit and him ending up in a wheelchair like my dad.

One week during practice, Colton's buddy James took a hit that left him in the hospital for weeks. James was a big boy, but an unexpected tackle from his blind side shattered his knee, splintering it into a reconstructive mess. After the surgery to repair the damage, he developed blood clots which made his recovery even tougher. He returned to school in a wheelchair, and later crutches, but never did regain full use of the leg. To this day he walks with a profound limp.

James was voted an honorary captain by Colton and the other captains, and limped out onto the field, arm in arm with the boys, as they gathered for the coin toss and other pregame rituals. Watching him only furthered my anguish, until I finally couldn't stand the fear anymore. I flooded my mind with Scriptures that assured me Colton was cared for, but it was a profound phrase that God whispered to me that changed my fear to trust: *"I will take him into the manhood I've designed for him."* Believing that God had Colton's manhood designed long before I started to worry about it somehow squelched the choking screams of fear that tormented me.

Colton played the last play-off games of his senior year with a broken wrist. After consulting with a doctor who works with professional hockey teams about whether Colton could play with a cast on (we went to the right kind of doctor to get a "yes," don't you think?), our boy wrapped his cast in bubble wrap and played. You've never seen a happier woman as the clock to their final game ticked down to zero and my son was still intact!

It's tempting to read stories of faith in the Bible, and forget that these men and women were sometimes fearful. Today we're going to spend time with a man who acknowledged his fear and bravely moved past it. Ananias lived in a scary time when believers were regularly taken from their homes, tortured, and killed for their faith in Christ. And to make matters worse, Ananias was about to go face-to-face with the most feared persecutor of all: Paul.

Please turn to Acts 9 and read verses 10–19.

Ananias obviously had a close relationship with Jesus because he knew exactly who was speaking when the Lord called his name. What did he say when Jesus called to him? Write his response below.

This response should have a familiar ring to it. Turn to the following Scriptures and write what Isaiah and Samuel said in response to God's call.

Isaiah 6:8

1 Samuel 3:1-10

Ananias was in good company. His intimacy with the Lord allowed him to hear a clear set of directions from Jesus that specified how he wanted Paul to regain his sight. Unfortunately, fear was about to make its snide entry.

 How did Ananias explain his fear to Jesus in verses 13-14? Did he have good cause to fear?

Often what we fear is real and scary. I hate when people belittle what we're afraid of by making comments like, "What's the big deal?" Jesus didn't belittle Ananias's fear; he acknowledged it because he knew it was a reality.

When I would explain my fear of paralysis from a football injury, some friends would look at me like I was ridiculous. But I had one friend, Tammy, who knew about my dad, and reassured me with prayer and encouragement.

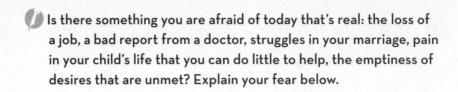 Is there something you are afraid of today that's real: the loss of a job, a bad report from a doctor, struggles in your marriage, pain in your child's life that you can do little to help, the emptiness of desires that are unmet? Explain your fear below.

Jesus respectfully let Ananias describe why he was afraid, but then uttered one word that evaporated fear's black landscape. Read Acts 9:15 and write the first word Jesus spoke in bold letters below.

We'll never get over fear if we don't go. Jesus understands what makes us tremble, yet he still says, "Go." The remarkable thing about Ananias is that he went!

How did Ananias speak to Paul, who incidentally was struggling with some fear himself after being blind for days (v. 17)?

Knowing that Paul had been the enemy, it's fascinating that the first words from Ananias's mouth when he greeted him were "Brother Paul." He had chosen to believe what Jesus said about this man rather than what his fear said, and that's where belief has its finest victory. I think there were two men who gained eyesight that day; both Paul and Ananias overcame their fear as scales fell from their eyes. Until tomorrow, sweet friend, may our eyes be free from fear's scales.

GOING DEEPER (OPTIONAL)

Let this story about fear ease any anxiety you feel today:

Charles Bowles's father was African; his mother was the daughter of a Revolutionary War hero. He was converted as a youth and called into the ministry. He was a black preacher in the far north who made waves and saved souls—but not everyone was pleased with his spiritual progress. In Huntington, Vermont, a mob secretly plotted to attack him at his next worship service. They intended to tie him to a wooden horse and plunge him into the lake to sink and drown. Bowles heard of the plot, and while the enemy was planning his weapons of destruction, Bowles was kneeling in a green grove, praying at the throne of his Redeemer. While the band of angry men were preparing with whiskey and cursing, he was preparing with praise and petition.

The service began, and the mob seated before him awaited their signal. Bowles read from Matthew 23:33 (NASB): *"You serpents, you brood of vipers, how will you escape the sentence of hell?"*

He preached with such fervor that no one dared move. He finished by saying, "I have been informed there are persons here who would like to put me on a wooden horse, carry me to the lake, and throw me in; and now, dear creatures, I make no resistance." He had only one request, and that was that on the way to the lake the assembly sing hymns. "Glory be to God! Yes, we will have music! Glory to God!"

He spoke with a powerful voice and such confidence in God that it moved like an electric shock through the congregation, and produced an effect upon the mob that could scarcely have been equaled if a bolt from heaven had fallen. They were so overcome that they all fell prostrate on the floor.

Shortly afterward, the troublemakers did meet Bowles at the lake—where *he* plunged *them* into its chilly waters, baptizing them as followers of his Lord Jesus.[18]

DAY FOUR THE HOLY TENSION OF EMBARRASSMENT

The other day, I was sitting at a baseball game watching the fans around me. (Don't tell my husband that I wasn't watching the game!) I couldn't help but notice a young couple obviously on their first date. They were performing for each other—telling jokes, laughing, playfully nudging each other's arms. Everything seemed to be going fine until the pretty girl took a bite of her hot dog and ketchup and mustard sprayed into her eyes! The more she rubbed them, the more she looked like a clown ready for a circus.

She was so embarrassed that she finally took a heap of napkins and ran for the ladies' room. When she came back to her seat, she was a little less playful. Actually, she was a bit shy—and I got the sense that embarrassment got the best of her. Embarrassment has a way of doing that.

My guess is that embarrassment has robbed us all of some finer moments. I know I've had my share of knee-slappers when it comes to looking stupid, but what really shakes me up is *spiritual embarrassment.* Deeper and more cutting than physical embarrassment, spiritual embarrassment has the power to snatch me away from God's glory. It dresses itself to look cute, but underneath the attractive exterior it's nothing but a bogus counterfeit to authentic belief. Let's peek into embarrassment's closet and see if we're wearing any of its latest designs.

- When God doesn't deliver the answers we hoped for after praying our requests publicly, we're embarrassed we made ourselves so vulnerable.
- When God moves or engages people in ways we don't understand, we feel as if we need to defend his reputation—or worse, distance ourselves from him so we won't be associated with questions we don't have answers for.
- Filled with confidence in most areas of life, when it comes to talking about Jesus we clam up, embarrassed that we may step on some pedicured toes.
- Going to church is great, but when asked to lead or volunteer in ways that place us outside our sphere of security, the answer is always an immediate "no thanks."

Unfortunately, I've worn some clothes from this closet—and so did one of my favorite men in Scripture—Peter.

Always a lover of drama, Peter was a man after my own heart. If there was action, he wanted in on it. Yet, as bold and in love with Jesus as he was, one of his toughest opponents was spiritual embarrassment.

Peter, like every other faithful Jew, had been waiting for a Messiah: someone who would sweep the political landscape and overturn the Roman government's power and abuse. He knew he had found this Messiah in Jesus, but toward the end of Jesus' life, the political coup wasn't playing out as Peter had imagined. When Jesus began talking about suffering, and eventually being murdered, Peter pulled him aside to let him know that this kind of talk was a bit embarrassing to the cause.

Turn to Matthew 16 and read verses 21–23.

What did Peter say to Jesus in verse 22 and how do his words reflect the state of his heart?

I'm sure Peter was speaking out of love for Jesus, but I also think he was a little embarrassed that a man he had given his life to serve was proclaiming he was going to die like a criminal. Jesus was supposed to be a heroic Messiah after all, not an insignificant nobody!

But Jesus slammed Peter's pride with a comment meant straight for its true author: "Get behind me, Satan!" Talk about putting Peter in his place. I bet he couldn't speak for the rest of the day!

Shortly after this incident, everything Jesus predicted came to pass. Peter found himself in the courtyard of the high priest, trying to stay warm—while inside Jesus was being beat up, made fun of, and spit on. This was embarrassing to say the least, and it was about to get even worse.

Turn to Mark 14 and read verses 66–72.

Name the people Peter was speaking to as three times he denied knowing Jesus. (I've done the first one for you.)

> Denial #1: *A servant girl*
>
> Denial #2: _____
>
> Denial #3: _____

Interestingly, it was common people asking a simple question who pushed Peter into a swamp of spiritual embarrassment. So often it's the same for us. It's the little situations that push us into the mud.

Can you relate? Maybe sitting at lunch with coworkers, afraid to tell them how God has worked in your life because they might think you're weird. Or afraid to share a need because God may not come through … and that would be embarrassing.

Below, write about a time you've been spiritually embarrassed. We all have at some point, so don't feel embarrassed to jot something down!

One of my biggest struggles with spiritual embarrassment came in a lesson I learned from my dad. After his car wreck I stayed distant from him, both physically and emotionally, for the next ten years. I couldn't wrap my mind around his pain, and I couldn't help but think that had he made different choices that night, our family may have had a chance at normalcy. So I did what any other adolescent might have done—I blamed him.

When, during college, I asked Jesus to take my life and save it, the first thing he showed me was the bitter thorns that had grown over the garden of my heart toward my father. I knew I had to let Jesus pick those thorns out, one by one. It wasn't pretty, as some were completely grafted into the soil of my spirit.

Each summer I returned home from college to work at a health club. My plan was to go see my father on the weekends. After my dad's wreck, he initially lived at home, but it became apparent that his medical needs were too great for my mom to handle, so he was moved to a small hospital in the little mountain town he had grown up in.

Our family shared one car between four drivers, so on Friday afternoon I would either take the bus or ride with my aunt to spend time with him. My grandparents had a home about a block from the hospital, so I always had a place to stay.

After the first few weekends, I began to feel a stirring in my soul. I finally mustered up the courage to tell my sister that I believed God was going to physically heal my dad. Though he had been in a wheelchair for years at this point, I was sure a healing was going to take place. What made this stirring even more dramatic is that I was engaged to be married in the fall, and I could picture my dad walking me down the aisle as I wore the dress my mom had worn on their wedding day. Confident that Dad would walk, I set about telling everyone I knew (and even those I didn't know) to start praying.

Each weekend, Dad and I would wheel around that town, basking in the Colorado sunshine as it warmed the green hills that nestled houses, shops, and the barbed-wire fences corralling distant cattle. I explained my newfound faith to my dad, as he listened intently, asked questions, and pondered my replies.

One day I just came right out with it. "Dad, I think God wants to heal you. I think he wants to restore your legs so you can walk again!" Nervously, I waited for his reply. Truthfully, I thought he might look at me like I was one crayon short of a box set, but instead he quietly asked, "Well, how do we go about this?" That was my signal that something big was about to happen.

Dad agreed to ask the nurses if he and I could use an empty hospital room the next morning. I told him I had no idea what this miracle might look like, but having a room to settle in seemed smart.

I didn't sleep a wink that night. I tossed and turned in a heap of sheets and blankets, anxiously waiting for the sun to come up on the day of healing.

As I walked into Dad's room, he informed me that the nurses said there was no space available, so we agreed to wheel down to my grandparents' house and sit in their garage. Surrounded by oil stains and lawn equipment, I opened my Bible to some Scriptures I felt were perfect for Dad. Suddenly, he began to weep. He asked me to read the story again about the paralyzed man who was lowered down from a roof to be placed in front of Jesus. Jesus said to this man, "Your sins are forgiven." That's where my dad seemed to lose it.

He asked me to pray with him, and there in that dirty garage he asked Jesus to heal him too. Immediately, I was ready for the good stuff. "Okay, Dad, now how about we pray for the healing of your paralyzed legs?" He looked at me with red eyes and said, "Sweetheart, I don't want you to think you didn't do everything you were supposed to do, because you have. My life isn't the same. But I have some things I need to work out personally with God, and I think I need to do it from this wheelchair."

I was stunned. Embarrassed. What about all the people I told that my dad was going to walk?

Dad asked me to come to his room later to highlight the Scriptures we talked about; for the moment, he wanted to take some time by himself to wheel back to the hospital. Frankly, I was relieved. I needed some time alone with God too.

I climbed into my grandma's orange Chevy Blazer and sped to the ranch they owned outside of town. The Colorado River runs straight through the middle of their land, so I parked the Blazer on a dirt driveway and ran toward a wooden bridge. Holding on to the rickety railing, I began to weep before God.

"I thought you promised to make my dad walk!" I sobbed. "Why didn't you heal my dad?" Crying turned to moaning and moaning turned to whimpers as I eventually quit screaming long enough to catch my breath. It was in that breath that I heard God's reply. "I *did* heal him."

Suddenly, it all made sense. Dad *was* healed. Some healings are *internal*, some are *external*, and some are *eternal*. Embarrassment seemed to wash away like the current of the river under the bridge.

Dad didn't walk me down the aisle at my wedding, but I knew his healing was nothing to be embarrassed of, and I was certain that I had been healed too. I was no longer embarrassed by the way God chose to love my dad—healing his heart and mind rather than his limbs. I was filled with pride for my earthly dad *and* my heavenly Dad the day I said, "I do."

DAY FIVE CURSING AND CASTING

I'm going to keep things short and to the point. I know I can get a bit wordy at times, but the Scripture we're studying today does all the talking.

Please turn to Matthew 21 and read verses 18 – 22.

Why do you think Jesus got mad at a fig tree?

The obvious reason is that it looked good from a distance — green and leafy — just like a tree would look if it were loaded with ripe figs. But when Jesus got close to it, he realized it was *only* green and leafy. No fruit to be enjoyed from this tree, it was only for show.

This Scripture is loaded with teaching potential on being real and growing authentic fruit in our lives, but I think there's a deeper layer of teaching that Jesus slid in the back door as he taught his disciples. I believe he was trying to show them that faith works two ways. We can have positive faith or negative faith. Often we have great amounts of negative faith in things we want changed for the positive.

What did Jesus say in verse 21 about the power of our words?

He followed this with a statement that bulldozes negative faith and unbelieving prayer. Write verse 22 below.

There's a reason Jesus said cursing leads to withering. Who can stand under the weight of negative faith without shriveling? But on the other side of the mountain an invitation bellows for us to believe. To say to our mountains, "Move!" and not budge until they do. To look unbelief in the face and say, "Get out!"

I love how the New American Standard Bible describes this mountain-moving scene.

"Truly I say to you, if you have faith and do not doubt, you will not only do what was done to the fig tree, but even if you say to this mountain, 'Be taken up and cast into the sea,' it will happen." (v. 21, emphasis added)

Essentially, we have two words to describe what we can do with our faith. We can either *curse* or *cast*. Often we don't even know we're cursing as we stand at the edge of our faith blurting out words like:

- My marriage will always be mediocre at best.
- I'll never live in a body I'm proud of.
- My health will never improve; it's downhill from here.
- I'll never find someone to love.
- I'll never be free from what consumes me.

Like a tree withered from the root up, this faith is rotten to the core. On the other hand, casting is alive, active, and aware. It speaks hope into a blur of uncertainty, and produces a fruit that's sweet and attractive.

Spend some time listing a few personal examples in the chart below and then prayerfully consider your overall cursing and casting tendencies.

Cursing (causing things to wither)	Casting (all things you ask in prayer, believing and receiving)

Now, take the things you've listed in the casting column and write them as a prayer below. Try to catch yourself today when you start to curse instead of cast. Remember the casting prayer you've written, and think about the power of your words. I'm right here with you, sweet friend, ready to duct tape my mouth when it chooses to curse instead of cast.

Session Five

LISTENING POSTURES

The other day I was talking to a woman who barely noticed I was speaking. Before I could get a sentence out, she was blurting a response right over it. Each time I tried to share a meaningful thought, she already had four stories of her own lined up, ready to tell. I was exhausted by the end of the "conversation." It felt like I had just run a marathon with weights around my ankles. It's no fun talking when people don't want to listen! Yet I know the woman I just described is often me—with God trying to get a word in edgewise.

Listening has a body language of its own, with certain nuances and postures that help an attentive ear truly hear. If listening has its own body language, there's no better way to understand this dialect than by studying the postures that promote an attentive ear. Our hearts hold internal attitudes conducive to hearing from God, while our bodies settle into physical positions that help us hear. Our capacity to listen is like a child learning to walk. Certain postures must be present if a toddler is to remain upright. Hearing from God also requires postures that help us take next steps. This week we're going to look at three of these postures: a humbling posture, a reviving posture, and an expectant posture.

How we listen *for* God can determine our filling *by* him. So many times I beg to hear from God, and sadly, when he tries to speak, I'm either talking over him or not paying attention. I want to listen to God like a lover listens to words from her beloved, a child listens to the words of a gentle mama, or a student listens to the words of a trusted teacher.

Listening is a dance where one leads and the other follows. Now, if I could just quit trying to lead and let God swing me around the dance floor without me stepping on his toes!

GROUP DISCUSSION (approx. 25 minutes)

Discuss the following questions based on the week four personal study.

1. Jesus spoke the words, *"All things are possible to those who believe"* at a critical time for the man who had a son struggling with seizures (Mark 9:23 NASB). Is it easier for you to believe God when you're in the midst of panic and fear, or is it easier for you to trust him when everything's running smoothly? Explain.

2. If *holy tension* is the tug-of-war we feel when our minds say, "I do believe, help my unbelief!" how can we move past the tug of unbelief toward the pull of belief?

3. Are you waiting for a "but Jesus" in your life (Mark 9:27)? Share what it is and why it's so important to you.

4. Day Two's personal study was about doubt. How did Naaman's doubt (and pride) almost rob him of healing (2 Kings 5)?

5. *Destructive doubt* centers around presumptions such as:

   • I'm not sure if God is good. If he's so good, why is there so much bad?

   • I'm not sure he cares deeply about the issues of my life.

   • I'm not sure his power supersedes the world I live in.

   While *productive doubt* sounds more like this:

   • I don't understand everything happening to me, but I trust that God does.

   • I choose to believe in the good character of God.

   • I will keep my eyes on Jesus rather than my circumstances.

Do you find yourself more prone to destructive doubt or productive doubt? Why?

6. In Acts 9, Jesus instructed Ananias to seek out Paul, a man known for hatred and brutality toward Christians. How did Ananias's obedience and trust outweigh the holy tension of fear? What can we learn from Ananias?

7. Day Four's personal study focused on some of the characteristics of spiritual embarrassment. If you struggle with any of these, give an example. Even Peter, Jesus' close disciple, fought embarrassment when it came to his faith. In what ways might we help each other fight such embarrassment?

8. Jesus cursed a fig tree that didn't have any fruit to illustrate that sometimes we have a great amount of negative faith in things we want changed for the positive. We curse spiritually and we cast spiritually. What's the difference between the two? What do you personally curse or cast?

9. If you have other insights or questions from last week's personal study, share them now as time permits.

VIDEO TEACHING (22 minutes)

Watch the video. The main points are included here for you. Jot down additional notes if you wish.

How we listen *for* God can determine our filling *by* him.

If we want to hear from God, we need to posture ourselves humbly and expectantly.

1. **The Humbling Posture**

   - This Pharisee in Luke 18:10–14 was praying to "himself"—spouting off how he was better than other people.
   - He then listed his spiritual resume.
   - The tax gatherer wanted God more than accolades. He knew he was a mess, yet he was the one God justified, not the Pharisee.

2. **The Expectant Posture**

   - Habakkuk 2:2–3 (NASB) tells us to "record the vision … that the one who reads it may run…. Though it tarries, wait for it, for it certainly … will not delay."
   - When we pray from a posture of expectation rather than defeat, God stirs up faith in us to believe he is bigger than any destruction.

PERSONAL STUDY

DAY ONE A HUMBLING POSTURE

To hear from God we must listen from a humble stance. If we're boastful, complaining, irritated, chatty—or fairly convinced that God is lucky we've chosen to grace him with our presence—we'll rarely hear his voice. He might orchestrate the occasional "knock down," where we get socked in the jaw with something he's trying to say to us, but typically God waits until we are humbly ready to hear.

I can always tell when my head noise is starting to get a bit sassy. You know what I mean, that running conversation you have in your head with God, your family, coworkers, or the person who's cut you off in traffic? Remember *Sassy Pants Girl* from our first week together? She isn't a good listener, because whenever God tries to speak, she either has an agenda of her own or doesn't have the maturity to zip up her mouth and tune in her ears.

Oh how I've worn the pants of Miss Sassy! And let's not exclude our male counterparts on this one. There's such a thing as Mr. Sassy Pants—his pants are just less stylish than ours.

My favorite Mr. Sassy in the Bible is Peter. He had serious wax in his ears, because instead of being a humble listener, he was often a knee-jerk talker. He found himself asking questions when he should have been listening, pledging allegiance to Jesus and then denying he knew him, and falling asleep when he should have been alert and praying. Most people would write off Peter as a failure, but Jesus considered him one of his best friends.

What's most impressive about Peter is that he changed. He became a good listener, one who knew how to wait upon God. After Pentecost, Peter was the mouthpiece of the early church. Unlike earlier in his life, he now humbly listened before he spoke. In one of his most quoted chapters, Peter boldly explains the necessity of being humble.

Please turn to 1 Peter 5:6–7. These verses have a seesaw effect when we look at the action we are to take and the action that God takes in our quest for humility. List what our roles are, and what God's roles are. The first one is done for you:

Our role (v. 6): *Humble yourself*

God's role (v. 6): _____

Our role (v. 7): _____

God's role (v. 7): _____

Sounds easy: just be humble and God will do the rest. But my daughter Brooke often brings me back to square one when she says, "Yeah but, Mom, what does it mean to be humble? How do we do that?" Good question.

Let's see if we can come up with some relevant examples:

- Instead of drawing attention to yourself in a group, you can give the spotlight to someone who is shy or unnoticed.
- When complimented, you can utter praise to the One who gave the talent or the looks—even if the praise is silently whispered in your heart.
- When tempted to think highly of yourself for whatever reason, consider other people as more important, even those that seem low on society's "A list." (This could simply mean making eye contact with all kinds of people, wishing them well, or praying for them as you rub against their lives.)
- Instead of defending yourself or trying to make yourself look impeccable, let the authentic "you" show through. A humble person is more inviting than a perfect one.

Is there something you'd like to add to this list? An idea, person, or environment in which you know you need the fresh breath of humility? Share it below.

In verse 7, Peter encourages us to cast our anxiety on the Lord, because the Lord cares for us. But Peter knows it goes even deeper than this. If we don't ... the devil will be prowling (v. 8). What does Peter instruct us to do in verse 9?

A ballplayer I greatly admire shares the story of how God resurrected his life and baseball career after they spiraled downward due to drug and alcohol abuse. As a brand-new Christian, he didn't know much about the Bible, but he knew one small phrase from 1 Peter that literally saved his life: *resist the devil*. It was enough to turn his whole life around.

I love how Peter adds a bit of comfort in verse 9 by reminding us that even if we think our problems are different, more serious, or harder to fix than anyone else's, believers all over the world are experiencing the very same trials.

After we've suffered for a little while, what does God do for us? Write out verse 10 below.

I remember when this passage became one of my favorites. Bobby had been the starting shortstop for the New York Yankees for two years, but after a bout of less than stellar performances, we had the sick feeling the Yankees were about to send him back to the minor leagues. Eight months pregnant with our second child, I remember coming home to find Bobby sitting on the couch in the dark. His eyes were red and his heart was deflated. He was used to being a star, the one everyone cheered for, leader of the pack. And now he was sitting in the dark wondering if he'd have a job the next day.

He did indeed go back to the minor leagues, and because I was a high-risk pregnancy I couldn't join him there until after the birth of our daughter. I remember reading these verses on humility like they were balm to sunburned skin. Each night I would recite them to Bobby on the phone, as together we begged God to make them real to us in our lives. God *did* make them real, as Bobby never again established himself as a starter in the big leagues after that disappointing season. But humility had a different purpose—a greater purpose—in the way he and I loved and cared for his teammates and their families. Not as "stars," but as servants. I'm convinced that humility is one of Jesus' favorite traits in those he loves.

Turn to Matthew 23 and read verses 1–12. How would you describe the religious people Jesus was talking about in these verses?

Verse 11 and 12 clarify that if we exalt ourselves (think of ourselves as better than other people), we will be humbled. He doesn't say we *might* be; he says we *will* be. I would much rather put myself in that position than have to be put there like a behavioral time-out!

Are there specific ways you can humble yourself in your marriage, at work, in friendships, in your community? What would this look like? Here's an example from my life that might get you started.

I ran into Starbucks to get a tea, and a young man I see there regularly cut in line in front of me. I was in a hurry—how irritating! I looked closely at him: baggy clothes, tattoos and piercings, and the scent of smoke so strong it could knock you back a few steps. Then I thought about how I see him there all hours of the day and began wondering if he might be using his laptop to job hunt. I also wondered if he might be a struggling writer (like me!), using a coffee shop as a getaway. I was reminded that I needed to get to an important meeting, but was slammed with the thought, *Why do I think my schedule is more important than his?*

So, instead of letting out an irritating sigh, I bought him a Starbucks gift card and placed it at his table as he sat down. I asked God to humble my still irritated heart — to turn that moment into a holy one instead of a huffing one.

(icon) **Now it's your turn. You might want to recall a time you showed humility, or try to think of a new opportunity in which you can display a humble posture rather than a self-seeking one.**

(icon) **How can this posture of humility help you hear from God?**

I love hearing stories about people humbly listening to God. It waters my soul in a land that exudes pride and self-conceit. So here's one I'd like to leave you with today.

It started on a bus in England. Gladys Aylward, a poorly educated twenty-eight-year-old parlor maid, was reading about China and the need for missionaries there, and from that moment, China became her passion. She applied to a missionary agency only to be turned down. Crushed with disappointment, she returned to her servant's room and turned her purse upside down. Two pennies fell on top of her Bible. "O God," she prayed, "here's my Bible! Here's my money! Here's me!" Gladys began hoarding every cent to purchase passage to China.

The journey was hair-raising and nearly cost her life. But eventually, Gladys reached China in the winter of 1932, showing up at the home of an older missionary who took her in — but didn't quite know what to do with her!

Yet Gladys became one of the most amazing missionaries of modern history. Her biography was made into a movie starring Ingrid Bergman. She dined with Queen Elizabeth II and spoke in great churches. She even became the subject for the television show *This Is Your Life*.

But none of this acclaim fazed her. She was used to humbly serving God, rather than being served. "I wasn't God's first choice for what I've done for China," she once said. "There was somebody else … I don't know who it was—God's first choice. I don't know what happened. Perhaps he died. Perhaps he wasn't willing. And God looked down and saw me."[19]

GOING DEEPER (OPTIONAL)

Every now and then I hear someone say, "She got a slice of humble pie." I love pie, especially when it's warm and pumpkin, but this is a different kind altogether. In God's kitchen, humble pie is made of just a couple of fresh ingredients: gentleness and unpretentious love. Digest the following verses on humble pie. They're truly delicious and won't make you fat!

Micah 6:8

Matthew 11:29

Philippians 3:21; 4:12

James 4:6

DAY TWO A REVIVING POSTURE

This morning I awoke with a question on my mind—one I've been asked hundreds of times by both men and women. It doesn't matter how seasoned someone is in their faith, this question still ranks in the top three in terms of confusion and frustration: *"How do I know if I've heard from God?"*

It's not an easy question to answer because God isn't a God of formulas. Sometimes he seems to stick to a script; other times, he writes it as he goes. His world. His prerogative.

Thankfully, we need not remain in a simmer of confusion. God *does* speak in several ways to those who are willing to listen:

- **The Bible:** God's written Word offers solid guidance to steer us through the challenges we face. Often, he answers us through words that jump off the page in relevance to our lives. A woman once told me she was considering having an affair and felt sure this was God's will for her life because she had prayed about it and felt peace. She said she heard God say, "Of course I want you to be happy; that's why I brought this man into your life." I responded by saying that what she *thought* she heard was in conflict with what we *know God has said in the Bible. I gave her a few passages to read in Scripture, and the next time I saw her she shared that she bawled her eyes out when she realized she hadn't heard from God at all, but had been deceived!*
- **Godly friends:** Sometimes God will reveal something to us through a friend's words or counsel. This still needs to be put through the strainer of God's Word, but often a friend can have a perspective we may be too blind to see.
- **Nature:** *For some, looking at the ocean, a mountain meadow, a field of flowers, a tree-lined hiking path, or a star-filled sky seems to usher in the whisper of God. Scripture says, "Since the creation of the world God's invisible qualities—his eternal power and divine nature—have been clearly seen, being understood from what has been made, so that people are without excuse" (Romans 1:20).*

- **Circumstances:** If you've prayed earnestly about something, and circumstances fall into place, you can assume you've heard from God. Bobby and I experienced this when we put our house on the market for the first time. It sat and sat with no offers. Eventually, we took the sign out of the front yard. Two years later, we relisted after praying about a course of events that God was orchestrating. The house sold in four days, and we got our asking price for it! We knew God was speaking.

- **A quiet, confident voice when you're praying:** Often this is referred to as "a still, small voice," but, truthfully, I don't think it's small or still. God's voice is confident and always lines up with his character. You may experience a confirmation, or a phrase may come to you that signals he is with you, listening to you. The prophet Isaiah described this voice when he wrote, *"Your ears will hear a word behind you, 'This is the way, walk in it,' whenever you turn to the right or the left"* (Isaiah 30:21 NASB).

Have you experienced hearing from God in one or more of these ways? If you are a veteran believer, which method seems to be the one God most often uses to speak to you? If you are a newer believer, is there a method you want to actively pursue?

Jesus plainly warns us to be careful listeners. He used one phrase in particular over and over to hammer home his point. Turn to Mark 4 and read verses 22–23. Write out these verses below.

It's funny how Jesus says, *"If anyone has ears to hear."* Don't we know that ears were made to hear? Yet he presses on this point to show that although we may have ears sticking out of the side of our heads, sometimes they aren't really listening.

Along with praying that *we* won't be hard of hearing, it's wise to pray that God will open *his* ears and hear the cry of our hearts. Turn to Daniel 9 and read verses 17 – 23.

🍃 **What did Daniel ask God to do in verses 17 and 18?**

🍃 **What did he beg of him in verse 19?**

🍃 **Notice the humble stance in which Daniel prayed in verse 20. What did he do?**

I'm stunned by the words in verse 23, uttered by the angel Gabriel: *"As soon as you began to pray, a word went out, which I have come to tell you, for you are highly esteemed."*

Have you ever wondered what happens in heaven when you pray? Imagine a "word going out" when you make your requests. This image sure changes the notion that prayer is boring or futile!

In the verses we've considered so far, we've seen Jesus telling us to have ears to hear what he's saying, and Daniel begging God to hear what he's asking. It's a two-way street as prayer and listening mingle like the breath that enters our mouth and leaves our nostrils.

🍃 **How would you rank your prayer life? Circle the number below that best represents how you pray and listen:**

4 You pray with utter belief that you are being heard. With confidence, you usher your requests to God and feel certain you'll get a response. You sit before him often throughout the day, praising him, listening for his whispers.

3 You pray with the belief you'll be heard, but sometimes it feels like you're talking to a tree stump. You feel confident you will eventually hear from God, and you know he's real, but it seems that other people may have a better method than you when it comes to getting answers from God.

2 You pray, but unless you see immediate results you wonder if God is listening or cares. Your prayer life consists of bursts of requests depending on what you need at the time. When things get better, you don't think much about praying or listening to God.

1 All this talk about God is intriguing, but prayer is for those who can't "do" and you are a doer. You've tried praying a few times in your life, but never got any results, so praying and listening seem futile, even a bit stupid.

Whether you're a four or a one on the above scale, rest assured that none of us is perfect. Even the most spiritual person you can think of struggles at times with praying and listening. As a matter of fact, sometimes I find my heart is in need of revival. Not the tent-shaking, people-on-the-floor type, but a personal place of quiet growth and desperate dependence.

Revival is a resuscitation of sorts. It's breathing air into depleted lungs. It's taking what's dull and unresponsive and bringing it back to life. Revival is being renewed, restored, refreshed, revitalized. The way I see it, revival is especially critical in three situations:

1. After we've failed God

2. After we've experienced heartbreak

3. When we feel spiritually dull or bland

It's in these slippery places that we often have the hardest time hearing from God, and certainly, praying to him. For the remainder of our study today, let's look at the first two on this list; tomorrow we'll examine the third.

Failing God carries with it the miserable stench of guilt and condemnation. God doesn't heap these treats on us; we seem more than capable of whipping them up ourselves when we realize what we've done. David was a man known for his love and commitment to God, yet he let God down in the worst way — through adultery, murder, and blemishing the heart of a woman that loved God too. Turn to 2 Samuel and read chapter 11.

Most people read this chapter with their eyes on David — after all, his nickname was "a man after God's heart." But I would like us to view the passage from Bathsheba's eyes. What do we know about her from verse 2?

Most scholars feel that David conquered Bathsheba like he conquered cities. He saw her, wanted her, and took her — regardless of the fact that she was married to one of his top military officials, Uriah. But what if she went willingly? What if secretly she admired the king and was flattered by his attention? How would this change the story?

How did Bathsheba react when she heard her husband had been killed in battle (v. 26)? From her reaction to the news, do you sense her heart breaking over the events that transpired?

It's when our hearts are broken that we most need them to be revived. Pain has a way of thrusting us into an emotional stupor. The more we feel pain, the more we hide from it, mask it, wallow in it, or pretend it doesn't hurt. It's in the midst of our wounds that we need a Savior to reach in and stroke the damaged tissue of our hearts. We need him to revive our brokenness.

At this point, she may not have realized that her husband died because of David's plan, but I can't help but wonder if she might have felt a bit relieved. How would you feel?

She quickly married David (v. 27) and you'd think the drama was finally over. But they were living in the middle of an oozing wound that needed to be scrubbed. The Lord sent the prophet Nathan to speak truth to David, and eventually David confessed his sin against the Lord and asked for forgiveness. But Bathsheba's pain was going to come in the form of childbirth. Read 2 Samuel 12:15–24.

How long did Bathsheba's child live (v. 18)?

David fasted and lay on the ground pleading with God before their child died. What do you think Bathsheba was doing during this time?

Verse 24 is what I call a *redeeming verse*. In one fragmented sentence we see a revival take place:

- David comforted his wife. They shared an intimate bond of repentance and reconciliation.
- He made love to her.
- She conceived and gave birth to a son they named Solomon.
- The Lord loved him.

If anyone let God down, it was this couple. David and Bathsheba had a relationship steeped in lies, deceit, and manipulative control—yet God not only redeemed them, he redeemed their love for one another.

As I ponder this story, I wonder about the ways we've let God down. Have you struggled with a habit you can't kick, a decision you made long ago and still feel guilty about, a relationship that drains you, feelings or words you're ashamed of—but don't know what to do with? Have you ever felt like you've let God down? Explain below.

The question I'd like to leave you with isn't, "Have you ever let God down?" because all of us can answer that with a resounding yes. The question I'd like you to savor is, "Can I flourish in a revival with God?" If revival is being renewed, restored, refreshed, and revitalized, may we choose revival over rebellion … and new life over stale indifference.

GOING DEEPER (OPTIONAL)

David and Bathsheba experienced a revival that brought their hearts back to God and to one another—but the pain that consumed them can be heard in David's poignant prayer for pardon recorded in Psalm 51. I often turn to this psalm when my heart needs stitches from wounds that continue to bleed. His words capture the futility of trying to mend ourselves and offer the hope of God's purifying hands. Slowly read this psalm aloud. (Reading out loud helps to focus on the words you're reading.) Write in your journal any portions of the psalm that speak to your life.

DAY THREE REVIVING FROM DULLNESS

Have you ever taken a bite of something that looked delicious, but tasted bland? No burst of flavor exciting your taste buds—just a boring monotony of chews and a swallow that covers a trail of mediocre. I hate that!

Truthfully, I'm disappointed with anything that seems boring or bland. Lectures, television shows, sermons, books, classes, moments that could be intimate but end up dull—all rank as high as cleaning the bathrooms in my book. But there's an area of my life that isn't just disappointing when it's dull—it's dangerous!—and that is my relationship with God.

I can always tell when I'm moving into a state of tasteless indifference. I can't hear from him, his Word seems cold and distant, and my prayers seem to bounce back in my face the minute they leave my mouth. How can a relationship with the God of the universe ever get boring? How can the living Christ seem like something from yesterday's menu?

The answer to that question lies in the essence of humanity. We live in the meadow of the mundane, not on the mountaintop of glory. It's in the meadow that we must seek the treasure of romping and roaming with a Savior. He is our lifeline. He is our safety and our thrill. He is the ultimate adventure. When our relationship with God seems to have hit the snooze button, I can assure you he hasn't changed—we are the ones who need to roll over and get out of bed.

A few years ago, I was doing a personal study of the Psalms. Each day I would read three of them, meditating on the words, and trying to fully digest the intensity of their meaning. When I reached Psalm 119, I felt like a panhandler who had just found gold. I didn't budge off that psalm for weeks. I read it and reread it. I journaled about it and took it apart in chunks. I even considered writing a book about it.

The author is raw with emotion, totally honest and compelling in his prayers. Maybe that's why I love this psalm. One minute he's thankful; the next he's weeping in distress. This is my kind of party.

Psalm 119 is long but powerful—each segment actually corresponds with a letter of the Jewish alphabet—so the first thing I'd like you to do is to read it through from start to finish. As you're reading, anytime you come across the word *revive*, make note of or circle it. Some versions use variations of the word: *restore, recover, renew*. In one of my translations (the New American Standard Bible), the word *revive* is used nine times!

Now let's carve a path of meaning from the psalmist's heart song. Look at verses 25-28, where the psalmist explains his state of mind—or things he has done—and also asks God to move in specific ways on his behalf. Write these in the appropriate columns below. (I've done a couple for you from the New American Standard Bible.)

The Psalmist	God
My soul cleaves to the dust	Revive me according to Your word
I've told of my ways	You've answered me

Verse 28 says, *"My soul weeps because of grief; strengthen me according to Your word"* (NASB). How does the Word (the Bible) renew strength that may be dull or lacking? After answering, write *the Word* in capital letters in the margin. We'll keep adding to this list as we continue our study.

Read verses 36–38 and write below what the psalmist asks God to protect him from.

Here the psalmist asks for his heart to be alive to God and not to dishonest gain. Most often, when we think of dishonest gain we think of money. This could be cheating on your taxes or failing to tell the cashier when you realize she's given you too much change. It might even look like withholding the truth from your spouse so he won't find out about a purchase or expenditure. Ouch!

Dishonest gain can also come from the gallows of gossip or self-promotion—elevating yourself while pushing someone else down. It's lying, fudging, or manipulating the truth in any fashion. I can't tell you how many times I've quoted this verse to myself when I hear rancid inner whispers encouraging me to lie.

A couple of years ago, I attended a Christian writers' conference where I tried to pitch the idea for my book *Spirit Hunger*. The short minutes a writer has with an editor can be nerve-wracking. One editor riddled me with questions about the sales of my first book, a niche title written for a small population of readers. He asked if I had sold a certain amount of books, and I quickly responded that I had, only to realize just as suddenly that the actual quantity was fewer. The next day I knew I had to find him and clarify my answer. No amount of gain is worth the dishonesty paid.

In verses 36–38, the psalmist also asks God to turn his eyes from vanity. But what is vanity? Here are a few words to describe it: pride, narcissism, arrogance, emptiness, hollowness, and worthlessness. I can think of a few reality television shows that fit this description. Funny how *that* kind of reality isn't God's reality.

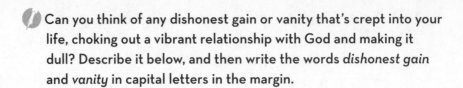 Can you think of any dishonest gain or vanity that's crept into your life, choking out a vibrant relationship with God and making it dull? Describe it below, and then write the words *dishonest gain* and *vanity* in capital letters in the margin.

Let's next look at verses 65–67. The psalmist asks for discernment (good judgment) and knowledge. It was the lack of discernment, he implies, that led him astray to the point that he was afflicted (troubled, brought low, humbled to recognize God's authority in his life).

Discernment is the shrewd ability to see people or circumstances in an unhindered way. It's the gift of clarity when everyone else is looking through tinted glasses. True discernment leads to knowledge, because when you see clearly, you know more. It's like turning on a light in a dark room. When the switch flips on, the darkness is gone.

How can discernment and knowledge revive our lives? What situations are surfacing in your life where you need discernment and knowledge? After you answer, write the words *discernment* and *knowledge* in capital letters in the margin.

Your workbook margins should now contain the words: THE WORD, DISHONEST GAIN, VANITY, DISCERNMENT, and KNOWLEDGE. So the questions we ponder are: How do we experience revival in these areas? How do we move from bland to powerful?

Nestled within the stanzas of this psalm are three secret keys capable of unlocking the prison of dullness. If we use these keys, something fantastic will happen.

 **Secret #1: Read verse 62 and write it out below.**

The psalmist says midnight, but it can be before you go to bed. Before you crawl under the sheet, bend down on your knees and give thanks to God. Your prayer doesn't have to be long or drawn out, but just commit to doing this for a week. That's secret #1.

Secret #2: Read verse 147 and write it out below.

If you don't do so already, commit to waking up early (for some it will be before dawn) and crying to God for help. Everything changes when you give time to God. Circumstances change; you change; anxiety shifts; fear subsides; spiritual adventures begin. That's secret #2.

Secret #3: This one's intense. Read verse 164 and write it out below.

Seven times a day the psalmist stopped to praise God. That may not seem like a lot, but when you're at work, or bustling through "to do" lists, praising God seven times a day will really get your attention. This is worship at its finest. Praising him no matter where we are or what we're doing, under our breath or at the tops of our lungs. Praise him, and watch what happens. That's secret #3.

Friends, can we commit to doing this together for a week? I can just picture all of us on our knees beside our beds at night, up at dawn, or praising seven times throughout our days. I'm glad the psalmist gave specific time frames instead of just saying, "Ask for help and be thankful." There's a reason he was so specific; I believe the reason is he knew his own tendency to wander! Remember, he wasn't backslidden or empty—he was in love with his God and *still* needed to be revived.

I know it may seem corny, but I wonder if you might join me in committing to these three secrets to revival. Please put your name before each commitment.

I, _____, commit to giving thanks before I get into bed for seven days.

I, _____, commit to rising early and crying to God for help for seven days.

I, _____, commit to praising God seven times throughout the day for seven days.

My hope is that seven days will turn into a month, and a month will turn into years of kneeling before bed, rising before dawn, and praising God with every breath we take. I'm writing this late at night, and can't wait to get on my knees to thank him tonight for you.

DAY FOUR AN EXPECTANT POSTURE – PRAYING WITH VISION

The other day I was having lunch with a good friend who uttered words that have scabbed over my life like a bad case of chicken pox. "I don't hear from God," she lamented. "I listen to you talk about hearing from God, but I'm not sure I ever have!"

We talked intimately as we ate our salads, reflecting on the most painful part of her life in which she needed prayer – her daughter. Repeatedly this daughter was making dangerous choices with men, alcohol, and drugs. Honestly, I had prayed with my friend countless times before, and couldn't remember her offering anything but trite, empty phrases to God when she prayed, nothing deeper than "Keep my daughter safe," or "Protect her." Although my friend's pain level was high, her expectancy level was low, and so she was stuck in a dead-end prayer cycle about as alive as a brown shrub.

Often, we don't hear God because we're not expecting anything from him – we have no vision. We're praying from a hundred random tangents, never focusing on anything specific, yet wanting specific results. The other end of that spectrum is praying for the same things in a routine manner. Crying out, "Protect my child" over and over, with no real request or vision as to how that protection might look.

Proverbs 29:18 says, *"Where there is no vision, the people are unrestrained"* (NASB). I've adopted this proverb personally to say, "When I pray with no vision, my prayers are unrestrained." My unrestrained prayers go to worst-case scenarios and tend to camp there, while unbelief seeps into the crevices of my hope that things can change.

What is vision? What does it mean to pray with vision rather than with defeat? Andy Stanley describes it like this:

> Visions are born in the soul of a man or woman who is consumed with the tension between what is and what could be. Anyone who is emotionally involved – frustrated, brokenhearted, maybe even angry – about the way things are in light of the way they believe things could be, is a candidate for a vision. Visions form in the hearts of those who are dissatisfied with the status quo.[20]

Is this you? Are you frustrated, brokenhearted, or even a bit angry about something in your life? Write briefly about it here.

Today is a difficult day for me to write. It's difficult because, in order to write it, I have to go back to a time when I prayed from the nasty banks of a filthy ditch. My praying was really worrying; my hope was fragile and weary; my mind seemed to run in sprints to hopeless hand wringing. If you've read my book *Spirit Hunger*, you know that I describe the following story in detail, but for our purposes today I'm going to share an abbreviated version, because this event was the catalyst for a revolution in my relationship with God.

We sent our oldest daughter, Brooke, to college with dreams as high as skyscrapers. She was going to her favorite college, studying something she had a passion for, and thrilled with her new life. But on Halloween night of her freshmen year, everything changed. She was drugged, sexually assaulted, and left to figure out the mess of confusion that now shrouded her thinking. By the time she came home for the summer, we were in triage mode as she shared her struggles with depression, alcohol, cutting, and bulimia. Some days I couldn't breathe as I watched the pain in her life pelt her like a hailstorm.

As a child growing up, we had a ditch that ran behind the fence of our backyard. It was nasty—full of snakes, muskrats, and leeches—but that didn't stop us from frolicking in it. I loved that ditch, even though I knew it wasn't the best environment to play in.

After several months of sleepless nights and worry-filled prayer for Brooke, God put the image of that ditch in my mind. I realized I was praying from the banks of that ditch, swept by the current of panic, faith-sucking leeches attached to my faith. God gently whispered, "Gari, do you believe I'm bigger than this destruction?" I mumbled back, "Yes. But I don't see how …"

The next day, as I combed my Bible hoping to get a shot of inspiration, my eyes landed on a portion of Scripture I had read many times before, but now leaped from the page with new meaning.

Please turn to Habakkuk 2:2 – 3 and write these verses below.

The New American Standard Bible uses the word *vision* to describe what the Lord asks the prophet to write down. Some versions use the word *revelation*, but I like the way *vision* sounds:

> Record the vision and inscribe it on tablets,
> That the one who reads it may run.
> For the vision is yet for the appointed time;
> It hastens toward the goal and it will not fail.
> Though it tarries, wait for it;
> For it will certainly come, it will not delay.

What does the prophet say we should do in verse 2? How is this different than praying randomly or routinely?

If you've ever prayed about something for a while and felt like you've seen little or no change, what does the prophet say about praying a vision prayer with regard to time?

After reading these verses, I felt like I knew what I needed to do—and that was to quit praying from a ditch of defeat and start praying with vision. Vision is just another word for hope. If we can muster up hope when we feel like we're floating down a ditch, we're on our way to a fresh encounter with God. I did as this verse instructs: I got a tablet and wrote my vision for Brooke on it. My vision looked like this:

- My daughter will be free of all that plagues her and will walk in the confidence and glory of Christ.
- She will have a husband who adores her heart and shares her love for God.
- Together they will minister hope and healing to those who struggle with heartaches from their past.
- She will use her talents, skills, and passion for film to flood God's love over a weary land.
- Jesus will be her comfort, strength, hope, and glory, and God's Word will thrive in her heart and mouth.

I added two or three Scriptures to this vision to solidify it in my heart. Often we hear about the value of praying Scriptures, but without a vision to accompany them, we're praying aimlessly.

Here's the difference between praying aimlessly (from a ditch) and praying with vision.

Ditch Prayer	Vision Prayer
despair, defeat, failure	hope, courage, faith
stuck reciting only what it sees	hopes in a God bigger than destruction
just scrapes by, surviving the days	excitedly looks toward the future
fearful, dreading, fretting	gutsy, tenacious, expectant

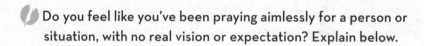 **Do you feel like you've been praying aimlessly for a person or situation, with no real vision or expectation? Explain below.**

Before we can run with the vision, we need to create it. Although doing so may seem awkward, it's a path toward expectation rather than defeat.

1. **Spill out to God everything that's on your mind regarding a person or situation.** Be specific and record these thoughts. Then reflect on how God might choose to touch and change this situation.

2. **Ask God to reveal your part in it.** What role do you play in this prayer? Sometimes you may only be required to pray; other times you may need to speak and encourage. Find two or three Scriptures to pray daily on behalf of your vision, and record them on the same tablet on which you've recorded your vision. It's important to stay tenacious in your belief, regardless of what you see going on around you.

3. **Note when you see God move in even the slightest way.** Many slight movements add up to miraculous change!

Now we are going to spend some time crafting *your* vision prayer. Your vision may regard a painful situation, or it may simply be something that surfaces repeatedly in the recesses of your spirit: the future of your children, the restoration of health, a job situation, our country, a broken marriage, troubled finances. Although I don't believe in formulas, I do believe in intentionality. Praying with purpose lifts us out of ditches and gives us direction.

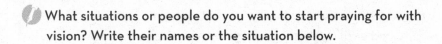 **What situations or people do you want to start praying for with vision? Write their names or the situation below.**

What changes would you like to see in this situation or person? (Dream big; don't let what you see now dictate what you hope for in the future.)

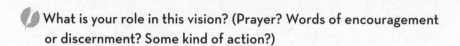 **What is your role in this vision? (Prayer? Words of encouragement or discernment? Some kind of action?)**

What two or three Scriptures support your hope in this vision? Write them out below.

Now copy your vision and the Scripture references in one place (a tablet, index card, chalkboard, the back of your Bible, your iPhone) so you can easily refer to it daily.

Sweet friend, I know I've asked a lot of you the past two days. Yesterday we took the Psalm 119 challenge by committing to pray with thanks before we go to bed each night, rising early in the morning to revive our minds in God's Word, and stopping to praise him seven times throughout our day. I wonder if we might add our vision prayer to this challenge. When you're praying before crawling into bed, remember your vision. When you're up early in the morning, pray it back to God before your day begins. And seven times throughout the day, pick one point from your vision and pray it as a praise to God for the work he is doing on your once fragile faith.

Whew! I get goose bumps just thinking about the power of God's women praying with expectant vision. Please don't skip this, with the hope to get to it later. Later is now! Don't let another day go by without positioning yourself in a new posture, with the vision to receive.

DAY FIVE BE STILL

So far this week, we've looked at various *internal* postures that aid our ability to hear from God. Today I'd like us to focus on a *physical* posture that invites listening—the invitation to "be still."

When my kids were young, I remember barking that phrase more times than I care to admit. Our life in professional baseball gifted me the pleasure of regularly driving across the country with the kids to meet my husband wherever he was playing or coaching. The phrase, "Be still," became my mantra as we traveled past countless Denny's and roadside truck stops. Here's how my monologue usually went: "Stop touching each other; scoot over and *be still*. If you can *be still*, we'll get a treat. Mommy needs you to *be still* so I can see where we're supposed to go. If you can *be still* for one more hour, I'll let you play at McDonald's. *Be still* so Mommy can hear herself think!"

Can you hear my theme (besides bribery)? Can you sense my desperation? If kids can be still when we ask, it's in those still moments that we can talk to them, without the commotion of their overactive voices and bodies!

I wonder if God gets tired of asking *us* to be still. The great thing about God is he doesn't bribe. He doesn't coerce us into being good listeners so he can have a moment to think. The only reason he asks us to be still is so that our physical bodies can catch up with our needy spirits. Our spirits long for intimate communion with the Father, so why is it so difficult for us to sit still and keep our hands to ourselves? The answer to this question seems to have three parts: we like to be busy, we like to talk, and we like to be in charge.

It's fascinating to watch how Jesus dealt with this. In two back-to-back chapters in Matthew he followed the same pattern to get a multitude of people to be still.

Please turn to Matthew 14 and read verses 13–21.

◊ After Jesus multiplied the five loaves of bread and two fish, notice what he had the crowd do in verse 19. Write this verse out below.

The Bible specifies that he had thousands of people sit down on the grass before he would feed them. Have you wondered why this was necessary? Why couldn't they eat standing up?

I believe Jesus' direction was more about listening to and watching him than finding a relaxing position in which to eat. The thousands gathered on the hill that day were probably huddled into groups of varying sizes. Some may have been watching Jesus from a distance, but in a group that large, everyone was probably doing their own thing, laughing, yelling, and meandering … until Jesus told them to sit down. Suddenly, men, women, and children quieted themselves and found a patch of grass to plop on. All eyes were on Jesus as he miraculously fed them not just fish and bread, but new life.

◊ Why do you think it was necessary for the people to sit down in order to receive? What would they have missed if they remained upright?

◊ Now turn to Matthew 15 and read verses 29 – 39. Write verse 35 below.

Here we see the same scene again. Jesus saw a need, and before he acted, he made sure the people were physically seated so they could see and hear what he was doing.

🍃 When Jesus asks *you* to "sit down," what does that typically look like? Do you usually listen?

In one man's life Jesus had to do more than make him sit; he had to make him blind.

Please turn to Acts 9 and read verses 1-19.

This is our friend Paul—the man who wrote a good portion of the New Testament. But before he was a believer, he had to be still for three days with virtually no eyesight.

🍃 What else did he refrain from in verse 9?

🍃 So with no sight, no food, and no drink, do you think Jesus had his undivided attention for a few days? What do you think Paul's prayers sounded like during those three days?

🍃 After Paul's physical silence, what happened after Ananias prayed over him in verse 17?

🌿 Paul had been a smart Jewish man bent on harming Christians and their dangerous view of God. It took him being blinded and silenced to finally learn how to see. Why do you think God had to go to such extreme measures to get Paul's attention?

🌿 What does he have to do to get your attention?

Tucked away in Psalm 46 is a verse that can virtually stop us in our noisy tracks. Please read it and circle the first two words below.

"Be still, and know that I am God ..." (v.10)

🌿 The word *still* used here is the Hebrew *raphah*, which means "to be relaxed, to not make an exhausting effort, or to be without anxiety over an issue." Try substituting any of these definitions into Psalm 46:10. I've done the first one for you below.

1. Be relaxed, and know that I am God.

2.

3.

Substituting these phrases sheds light on the depth of this verse. Being still doesn't come naturally to most of us. Think about it—we're born crying and then spend a good part of our lives after birth talking, moving, and figuring things out. To be still seems to go against the grain of who we are. Yet it's in stillness that we listen, and in listening that we change.

Session Six

WHO'S in CHARGE?

After teaching elementary school for almost two decades, I came to realize one important fact: kids will always try to figure out who's in charge. If the teacher's not in charge (too weak, too scared, too intimidated), then somebody in that room will take over. Usually, it's the student with the loudest voice and the meanest temperament!

Adults are no different. We walk into meetings or gatherings and try to size up who's running the show. Leaders and followers are God's design; I think that's why Jesus spent so much time talking about sheep and shepherds.

It's no accident that sheep are the following type. They'd follow each other right off a cliff if they didn't have a shepherd to stop them. But even with their tendency to follow, the redeeming quality of sheep is that they know how to listen to their shepherd. A shepherd can speak in no more than a whisper, and his sheep will obey his command. Just as a shepherd is in charge of his sheep, so God is in charge of us.

The other day I laughed my head off at something my friend Marvin had us do in the class I coteach on Sundays. He told us that one of his favorite foods is nachos, and then proceeded to describe the flavor and ingredients of the tasty snack his wife often makes for the family. After he had all of our mouths watering, he instructed us to repeat the word *nachos* after every phrase he said. (You have to say the word *nachos* with a bit of Southern twang to get the full meaning — still a chore for this Colorado girl!)

"The battle is mine …" then we said *nachos*!

"The direction of your life is mine … *nachos*!"

"The power in your life is mine … *nachos*!"

Does anyone else think that's hysterical? I may be a bit warped, but I love it! Those three phrases and the nachos that follow say it all. God's in charge. He's the boss. And the strength of your life is his … *nachos*.

GROUP DISCUSSION (approx. 25 minutes)

Discuss the following questions based on the week five personal study.

1. In order to truly hear from God, we must posture ourselves in a humble stance, but what does a humble posture look like? How does living in humility differ from the world's push to promote yourself whenever you can?

2. Jesus tells us, *"Whoever exalts himself shall be humbled, and whoever humbles himself shall be exalted"* (Matthew 23:12). This indicates that we can either choose to humble ourselves, or resist this choice and have to be humbled by God. Has God ever humbled you? What did it look and feel like? What did you learn from that time of humility?

3. Gari mentioned several ways we typically hear from God: the Bible, godly friends, nature, circumstances, and a quiet confident voice when we're praying. How have you experienced hearing from God in any of these ways? What is the typical way you seem to hear from him?

4. This week's personal study talked about revival being a renewal and restoration. Typically we need revival after we've failed God, experienced heartbreak, or feel dull or bland in our relationship with him. Which of these seem to be the hardest to overcome in your life? What do you do to overcome them?

5. Psalm 119 is a cry for revival. The psalmist asks to be revived from dullness, the desire for dishonest gain, and vanity, and to recognize the need for discernment and knowledge. Do any of these items stand out as something for which you need revival?

6. Why is it crucial to pray with vision and expectation rather than in random tangents? How does a vision prayer differ from praying in a ditch?

7. Share your vision prayer with the members of your group so that they can join you in your vision of hope.

8. Why is our *physical* posture as well as our *internal* posture important when it comes to hearing from God? What physically gets in the way of you hearing from God?

9. If you have other insights or questions from last week's personal study, share them now as time permits.

VIDEO TEACHING (21 minutes)

Watch the video. The main points are included here for you. Jot down additional notes if you wish.

God uses a metaphor repeatedly in the Bible to describe his relationship with us. It's the picture of a potter and clay (Jeremiah 18:3 – 6).

Pottery Principle #1: We don't want to be the clay; we want to be the potter.

- Jonah is a good example of this. He ran away after God told him what he wanted him to do.
- He had a "potter and clay moment" in the belly of a fish when he realized he couldn't outrun God.
- God will equip us for every good work (Hebrews 13:21). If he calls us to do something, he will equip us to be able.

Pottery Principle #2: We want to look like other pots.

- We look at other types of pots we think we want to be, instead of growing into the pot he has made us.

Pottery Principle #3: We want the process of becoming useful to be painless, quick, and explainable.

- Pain is often the best road map to growth.
- When Jesus performed a miracle with clay in John 9, he spit on dirt and placed his "holy spit" on the blind boy's eyes. Those watching this miracle tried to figure out who sinned and why pain was present in the boy's life. Jesus explained that it was so the glory of God could be showcased.
- We curse the pain in our lives, but it's through that pain that Jesus teaches us to see.

PERSONAL STUDY

DAY ONE MOLDED LIKE CLAY

When I was young, my sister and I could entertain ourselves for hours with Play-Doh. There was nothing more exciting than picking just the right color and opening the lid to endless creative possibilities. We would cut, shape, and mold the dough until it resembled something familiar. My favorite things to make were replicas of food. I can still see the hamburger I made, complete with bun and filled with pickles, cheese, and tomatoes. With the pinch of clay or cut of a plastic knife, I could change, switch, or add to my masterpieces. And sometimes I balled up the dough and started over when I couldn't get it just right.

It's interesting that in the Bible, God repeatedly chose the image of a potter and clay to describe his relationship with us. Jeremiah 18:6 says, "*'Like the clay in the hand of the potter, so are you in my hand,' declares the LORD.*"

He's the potter and we're the clay. He shapes, molds, pinches, and creates—and sometimes he starts over just when we think our clay is either perfect or too messed up.

The problem with this powerful image is that we don't always want to go along with it. I believe if clay could talk, it'd be barking out orders as to how God should shape it. Sound strangely familiar? This leads me to what I call Pottery Principle #1: *We don't want to be the clay; we want to be the potter.*

One man in the Bible who illustrates the uncomfortable process of being shaped wasn't poor, needy, in trouble, or hurting; as a matter of fact, he was a king—Nebuchadnezzar of the empire of Babylon. Though his story is also told in 2 Kings, 2 Chronicles, and Jeremiah, we're going to follow his life through the book of Daniel.

Please turn to Daniel 1 and read verses 1–5.

What did Nebuchadnezzar do in Jerusalem? What, along with articles from the temple, did he take from the city?

Daniel and his three close friends were captured and trained for the king's service. It didn't take long for God to begin a potter-and-clay progression of events in the king's life. We'll break the time line into four incidents from which we can learn, looking at the first two incidents in Nebuchadnezzar's life today, and the others tomorrow. I know these two days are a bit heavy on Scripture reading, but I promise it reads like a thriller!

Nebuchadnezzar's First Dream

Turn to Daniel 2 and read verses 1–13.

In Daniel's day, dreams were considered messages from the gods, and the wise men of the kingdom were expected to interpret them. Usually they could give some sort of interpretation as long as they knew what the dream was about. But Nebuchadnezzar could not remember the dream because it had been sent by the Hebrew God and could only be understood by a servant of that God.[21] Of course, the Chaldeans (his magicians and astrologers) weren't servants of God, and therefore couldn't understand the dreams. Nebuchadnezzar certainly wasn't known for his patience and he threatened these fake interpreters with their lives.

What did Daniel do when he heard about the king's antics (vv. 16–24)?

What was his first line of defense when faced with an overwhelming challenge (vv. 17–18)?

We should never underestimate the power of asking people to pray for us when we're in need. It not only paved the way for God to move through Daniel, but it calmed his nerves in the midst of a panicking group of Chaldeans. After a night of prayer, God revealed to Daniel what no one else had been able to see. Read Daniel's interpretation of the dream in verses 31–45.

Starting in verse 36, Daniel laid out what would eventually be the demise of the Babylonian Empire and the series of empires (Medo-Persian, Greek, and Roman) that would follow.

Finally, in verse 44, Daniel foretold yet another kingdom. Write the verse below and explain whose kingdom Daniel was speaking of.

Daniel was telling this unsuspecting king about the kingdom of Christ—which thousands of years later still has no end! What was King Nebuchadnezzar's response to this conversation with Daniel (vv. 46–48)?

That was the first time this king acknowledged God. Sadly, acknowledging God and living for him are two separate things. The second time the king acknowledged God came at a high price for the friends of Daniel, because they had to sit in flames of fire for the king to experience a singe of understanding.

Three Men and a Furnace Fire
Read Daniel 3:1–18 and respond to the questions below.

What did the king set up on the plain of Dura?

Why did Shadrach, Meshach, and Abednego refuse to bow to this image?

Some readers may wonder where Daniel was when his friends were under such scrutiny for not worshiping this image. Some scholars believe he was attending to the king's business elsewhere, because we know that otherwise Daniel would have been shoulder to shoulder with his friends in the furnace.

The response of these three men to King Nebuchadnezzar's threat is one of my favorite in the Bible. Please write out Daniel 3:17–18 below.

It's the mature believer who can live out the true meaning of these verses. In essence, Daniel's friends said, "God can make all of this go away and save us from this situation, but even if he chooses not to—he's still God."

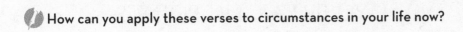 **How can you apply these verses to circumstances in your life now?**

Let's close our time today as we watch the Master Potter mold the clay of Nebuchadnezzar's life in an unusual way. Read Daniel 3:19–30.

Early in this section, the king raged in fury as his pride negotiated the fate of the young men (v. 19). But after witnessing their miraculous rescue, he blessed the God they trusted (v. 28).

Tomorrow we'll pick up where we left off in this potter-and-clay showdown.

DAY TWO BREAKING POINTS

I've always believed that people have breaking points—those moments of pressure and revelation when we either give in or stand up, but can no longer function the way we did before. As we saw in our study yesterday, King Nebuchadnezzar was beginning to break. For the second time, he had to acknowledge that a God unlike the gods he was used to had shown himself to be real.

Yesterday I explained that Nebuchadnezzar experienced four incidents that defined his understanding of the living God. The first was Daniel's interpretation of his dream; the second was his response to watching Shadrach, Meshach, and Abednego in the fire. Let's jump right into the Scripture today, because you're not going to believe how bizarre the next two incidents get!

A Second Dream Is Interpreted
Turn to Daniel 4 and read verses 4–8.

What does Nebuchadnezzar say in verse 8 to indicate that although he encountered the power of the living God before, there was no lasting change?

Remember how the king praised God after releasing Shadrach, Meshach, and Abednego from the fire? I really thought it was a turning point, but instead, it was merely a flash point—a moment that flashed before his eyes with the hint of recognition but no conviction of change. There's one thing Nebuchadnezzar *was* sure of, and that was the fact that Daniel could interpret dreams. Like a child who crawls into bed with Mommy and Daddy after a bad dream, the king wanted to crawl up next to Daniel and feel safe. But Daniel had anything but safety to offer him, once he knew what the troubling dream represented.

Read verses 10–26. What does Daniel say in verse 25 that sums up the meaning of the entire dream?

Daniel was so upset by the dream that he offered the king some godly advice. What was it (v. 27)?

Unfortunately, King Nebuchadnezzar still hadn't reached his breaking point.

Walk Like an Animal: Understanding at Last
A full year after this dream and troubling prophecy, the king was strolling around his rooftop, basking in his own glory, when the fulfillment of the words Daniel spoke twelve months earlier begin to take root.

Read Daniel 4:28–33.

Describe what this time was like for Nebuchadnezzar. What did he look like? What did he eat?

The king's pride led to a bout of mental illness so severe that he literally acted like a wild animal. Suddenly, at the end of seven years, Nebuchadnezzar's sanity was restored, along with his kingdom. He finally uttered words that reflect his understanding of this God he formally gave mere lip service to.

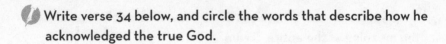 **Write verse 34 below, and circle the words that describe how he acknowledged the true God.**

Verse 37 could be called Nebuchadnezzar's "life verse" as, at last, he truly comprehended that God *"is able to humble those who walk in pride"* (NASB). Because pride was the wall that barricaded him from the presence of God, it had to be knocked down in order for him to understand.

I know in my own life there was a wall that kept me from experiencing God; that wall was insecurity. God had to dismantle this wall brick by brick, as my strength and courage grew in spite of the insecurity that used to rule my thoughts and beliefs.

Is there a wall that God is trying to bring down in your life, a barricade that needs to fall before he can raise something new? Describe it here.

We've chronicled the life of a king who learned how to be clay in the hands of the Potter. It didn't happen overnight for this king, but it may have transpired a bit more easily if he had let God have his way sooner. Sweet friend, let's not waste another minute trying to shape ourselves. Only our capable Potter sees the vessel he wants us to be — strong and useful in his collection of beauty.

DAY THREE "BUT I WANT TO LOOK LIKE THAT POT!"

Yesterday I talked about Pottery Principle #1: We don't want to be the clay; we want to be the potter. Today I'd like to introduce you to Pottery Principle #2: *We want to look like other pots.*

You don't have to look beyond the checkout stand magazines at the grocery store to see that women in America are dissatisfied with themselves. It may be a minor issue (cellulite on the thighs, wrinkles around the eyes, limp hair) or it may be a major shortfall (obesity, body hatred, wanting someone else's life). Whatever the case, we're hurting.

I've come to the stark realization that women need women, and frankly, we need God to redefine the standards by which we measure our worth. I know that when I dress for a meeting or a class, I'm dressing for my girlfriends more than anything else. I want to hear them say, "Cute outfit!" or "I like your hair!" One compliment can keep me charged for days in the "feeling good about myself" department.

I've adopted a new pattern of behavior the last few years. Every time I see something attractive in a woman — something she wears, says, or does — I compliment it immediately, to her face. I know there have been many surprised women when I've rubbed up next to them and told them I love their scarf, or the way they treated the salesperson. Why shouldn't we cheer each other on? It's too lonely not to.

Yet even though I long to cheer my fellow gender mates, I also have a tendency to look at them and want what they have. Thicker hair, prettier home, more time for relaxation, more money — it's a tug-of-war match that will leave our hearts blistered if we don't pay attention to its destructive pull.

This tug and pull of jealousy isn't new; as a matter of fact, it's part of the reason God calls himself the potter and us the clay. He reserves the right to make us as he sees fit. Listen to the words of the apostle Paul as he conveys a message that explains this struggle:

But who are you, a human being, to talk back to God? Shall what is formed say to the one who formed it, "Why did you make me like this?" Does not the potter have the right to make out of the same lump of clay some pottery for special purposes and some for common uses? (Romans 9:20–21)

As I ponder these verses, I'm reminded of the times I have a tendency to feel a pang of jealousy. Typically, it's when it appears someone else's life is being used for "special" purposes and mine is as common as a beige crayon. Nothing puts a woman into tug-of-war as quick as feeling plain.

I love to watch my two-year-old granddaughter twirl in her princess dress—full of delight and vigor. I'm sure she thinks she's the most treasured gift on earth, and of course, in my eyes she is. But it won't take long for her to realize she's just another student in a class picture, another number on the roll-call sheet, another pretty face.

What do we do with this mess? How do we unravel the desire to matter, to stand out, to be beautiful—without becoming an ego-saturated basket case?

Please turn to 1 Peter 3 and read verses 3–6. Write verse 4 below.

For years I kept my distance from these verses, mainly because I'm not a quiet person—and I thought verse 4 was saying I needed to be quiet in order to be pleasing to God. One day, in a tizzy over it, I asked God to help me understand the meaning of these verses. I was thrilled to realize he wasn't saying I had to be a quiet person, but rather, to have a quiet spirit before him. A quiet spirit before God is one that doesn't tell God how to run the show, but sits and listens for his words and embrace. It isn't proud or boastful, but instead, understands that anything good in us is a direct result of his favor.

Several versions of verses 3–4 paint broad strokes of meaning against the canvas of our lives.

Your adornment must not be merely external—braiding the hair, and wearing gold jewelry, or putting on dresses; but let it be the hidden person of the heart ... (NASB)

Your beauty should not come from outward adornment, such as elaborate hairstyles and the wearing of gold jewelry or fine clothes. Rather, it should be that of your inner self ... (NIV)

Don't be concerned about the outward beauty that depends on jewelry, or beautiful clothes, or hair arrangement. Be beautiful inside, in your hearts, with the lasting charm of a gentle and quiet spirit ... (LB)

It's the hidden, inner beauty that God enjoys—the kind of beauty that loves instead of criticizes, encourages instead of tears down, protects instead of gossips. What a relief that this kind of beauty has nothing to do with outward appearance!

It's interesting though, that of all the women Peter could use as an example of this type of beauty, he picked Sarah (v. 6). Let's look back at a few things we know about her.

 Turn to Genesis 12:11, 14. How is Sarai (Sarah) described in these verses?

She must have been stunning, because not once, but twice, Abraham lied about her being his sister to save his own life. The custom during his day was that the wife of a man could be taken for a ruler's pleasure, and the husband of the wife killed in return. Two separate times she was taken from Abraham and mistaken for his sister; so we know for certain Sarah was supermodel status. Some women hold the view that it's sinful to try to look beautiful. As if beauty is a bad thing and homeliness is a good thing. But Peter complimented Sarah's faith, fully knowing that she was gorgeous on the outside.

It's also worth noting that Sarah didn't always deal with things quietly or in a saintly way. Remember the mess with Hagar (Session 1)? Sarah was consumed with envy toward women with children, and when she couldn't conceive, she offered her maid to her husband. After Abraham slept with Hagar and got her pregnant, Sarah was mad at everyone involved, including God. Hmmm, doesn't sound sweet or mild mannered to me!

So what was Peter complimenting? What quality of beauty did he see in Sarah that he encourages us to model? It's the inner measure of respect she showed for her husband. Some translations use the word *submission*, which in certain circles is better known as the "s" word.

What's your first reaction to this word? Have you heard it before? Does it make you uncomfortable?

Submission isn't the sign of an old-fashioned woman or a weak one; it's the same word used to describe how Jesus lived his life on earth—submissive to his Father's will. One commentator defines submission as "voluntarily cooperating with someone else out of love and respect for God and for that person."[22]

This is an inner beauty unstained by the flawed flesh of men, or the controlling agenda of women. It's not to be mistaken for being a doormat for an insensitive spouse, but rather, a choice to respect rather than dominate, and to love rather than scorn.

Think for a minute about your own life. Is it difficult for you to submit to a husband—to a boss—to God? Why?

If we are clay, and God is our potter, he may want to shape us differently from the pot sitting next to us. Isn't this a submission of sorts? We can wiggle, scream, complain, and try to take ourselves off the spinning wheel God uses to shape us. In the long run, if we love him and are called according to his purposes, we're better off letting him do the shaping. The result will be real beauty, from the inside out.

GOING DEEPER (OPTIONAL)

Read Jeremiah's account of the potter and clay in Jeremiah 18:1–6.

Think about the fact that the clay was *spoiled* in the potter's hands, causing him to remake the entire vessel. What do you think being spoiled looks like? Why does God lovingly remake us when we are spoiled?

DAY FOUR "PLEASE, GOD, DON'T LET IT HURT!"

Do you love pain? Do you wake up in the morning saying, "I can't wait to feel miserable today"? I don't know a soul who would answer yes to these questions. As a matter of fact, most of us go to great lengths to avoid pain. I know the motto in athletic circles is, "No pain, no gain." That sounds noble and brave to an athlete, but I can tell you that most of us could rewrite that statement to say, "No pain, forget the gain!" Because, truthfully, as Pottery Principle #3 suggests, who wants to feel bad?

Pain has many outfits. Some are flirty and don't make much of an impact; while others profoundly affect us, as if we're wearing all black. Pain's darkest wardrobe has clothes perched on hangers we'd rather ignore: losing a loved one; debilitating health issues; loving a lost child; financial burden and stress; addiction; abandonment and betrayal; sexual, physical, and mental abuse — need I go on? Like the sound of fingernails scraping a chalkboard, pain causes us to flinch and cover our ears.

In one of God's greatest ironies, though pain causes sorrow, that sorrow can cause growth if met with open surrender. If I didn't see this irony play out repeatedly in my own life, I might think my last statement was just another trite saying to make sense of things we don't enjoy. Kind of like, "Eat your spinach so you can be strong!" Who cares about being strong when you're about to eat a leaf that's green?

There's a story in the Bible that has the guts to make sense of pain. Jesus went after pain like a doctor giving morphine, except his remedy had no ill effects.

Please turn to John 9 and read the entire chapter.

🍃 **How long had this man been blind (v. 1)?**

How did the disciples try to make sense of his pain (v. 2)?

Has anyone ever spoken insensitive words to you when you were hurting, as if they were trying to make sense of your pain? If so, describe the experience.

Please write out verse 3 below.

Sweet friend, here is one of the most powerful statements about pain we'll ever hear. Jesus in essence said, "Some of the painful things you experience are so the works of God might be displayed in you."

Does God take pleasure in the heartache and agony you experience in your pain? Goodness no! That's Satan's territory of sin and destruction. But God can display his works through these times if we aren't blind to his touch in the midst of them.

What did Jesus do with the clay he created (v. 6)?

It's interesting that Jesus didn't immediately heal this man. After placing clay on the man's eyes, what did Jesus tell him to do (v. 7)?

This verse starts with "Go!" We seem to keep running into this word in Scripture. Sometimes we think Jesus will do all the work, magically erasing any residue of pain, when actually he wants *us* to have a part in the growth. He wants us to understand that his works will be displayed if we have the guts to "go."

🍃 What was the fallout from this man's healing (vv. 13–34)?

🍃 Have you ever experienced a fallout after seeing the works of God displayed in your life (for example, friends or family not understanding, people you thought would be supportive ignoring you, feeling alone rather than surrounded by love)?

🍃 Jesus didn't say, "You're in pain ... deal with it!" or "I worked in your life, now you're on your own!" Read verse 35 and write it out below.

I love this verse because it says Jesus went to find this man. Jesus finds *us*. He finds us and helps us make sense of the work he has done in our lives—work that displays his glory.

In an intimate conversation with a man who now had sight, Jesus explained that it was the Pharisees who were blind (vv. 36–41). Suddenly, a lifetime of blind pain made sense and gave birth to growth.

If pain births sorrow, and sorrow births growth—then it's through this process we become useful. Oswald Chambers, in his devotional classic *My Utmost for His Highest*, beautifully explains sorrow's purpose:

> Sorrow burns up a great amount of shallowness, but it doesn't always make a man (or woman) better. Suffering either gives me myself or it destroys myself. You always know the man or woman who has been through the fires of sorrow and received themselves. You are certain you can go to them in trouble, and find they have ample leisure for you. If you receive yourself in the fires of sorrow, God will make you nourishment for other people.[23]

I used to run from pain, as if I could outwit it, as if I were fast enough to escape its embrace. Now I submit to it, because I know my Potter is the One who uses all the clay in my life to make a useful pot. Here's a thought to ponder throughout the day: Have you received yourself in the fires of sorrow, so that you can be nourishment for other people? That's how the works of God are displayed.

DAY FIVE THE LOOK OF A DISCIPLE

After more than thirty years in professional baseball, Bobby and I can usually spot the prototypical ballplayer: muscular, in shape, driven, focused. Of course, every now and then we run into a player who has us scratching our heads. "Sure doesn't look like an athlete," we say. But that's rare, because athletes typically have characteristics that distinguish them and set them apart.

This realization makes me wonder, "What do disciples of Jesus look like? What characteristics make them stand out from the rest?" I used to put the word *disciple* into the category of "holy people," men and women worthy of full-body halos. That was until I became one.

Synonyms for this lofty word include *follower*, *believer*, *supporter*, *devotee*, and *pupil*. Nowhere on the list do you see *perfect*, *unspoiled*, *impeccable*, *flawless*, or *faultless*. Indeed, the description of a disciple is more about being a learner than anything else. A person committed to Jesus — and committed to change.

Remember at the beginning of this study, I said that though we may read lots of Christian books, listen to many sermons, or regularly attend classes — unless we're changing, it doesn't matter how many times we flirt with God, we'll never be his disciples. Flirting is for those who stay shallow, while discipleship is the essence of intimacy.

So, as we close this study, I would like to ask you to follow a path of intimacy that leads us back to the very reason we've gathered: to be changed by a Savior and become a learner of his ways.

Please turn to Luke 10 and read verses 38 - 42. I know this is a passage that many Bible teachers have taught, but we are using it only as a springboard for where we'll end up today.

How would you describe Martha and how would you describe Mary?

Mary and Martha's brother, Lazarus, isn't mentioned in this Scripture, but we know that he and Jesus were also close friends, and that Jesus always made a point of stopping by their home in Bethany whenever he was nearby. If we were to compile a list of what we think each of these friends of Jesus were like when they first began to know him, it might have looked like this:

Martha: organizer, worker, driven, motivated, controller, liked to have her ducks not only in a row but sitting in a forward position

Mary: listener, dreamer, lounger, good at giving ideas but not executing them

Lazarus: holder of tradition and custom, listener, social (as he often sat at gatherings or held them at his house)

Late in Jesus' three-year ministry, Lazarus got severely ill, and even though Martha and Mary sent for Jesus to help, Lazarus died. By the time Jesus arrived in Bethany, Lazarus was already in the tomb.

Turn to John 11 and read verses 1–46.

 **Who was the first to come to Jesus in verse 20?**

Interesting that the sister who had held on to every word spoken by Jesus in our earlier Scripture chose to stay home, while the busybody superwoman went out to Jesus to hear what he had to say. It appears as if Martha was experiencing a change in her relationship with Christ … a softening and letting go of sorts.

 **What was Mary's attitude when she finally joined them (v. 32)?**

After spouting some words at Jesus regarding his poor timing, Mary broke down and cried. The sight was so moving that it brought Jesus to tears. But he wasn't through with this family yet.

 **What did Jesus command the dead brother to do in verse 43?**

Jesus told Lazarus to come out of the grave. Lazarus had to get up and move even though his eyes, hands, and feet were bound by wrappings that required trust in the Savior—not trust in his own unwrapping skills. He had listened to his teacher before. He had sat at the table with him and learned. Now he *had* to be changed by his master's teachings and have the guts to "come forth," or all of his learning was for empty show.

What happened as a result of this family's disciple-shaped hearts (vv. 45 – 46)?

Now we come to a place in Scripture where we can mark their growth as disciples. Read John 12:1 – 3 and fill in the following blanks:

Martha was _____ (v. 2)

Lazarus was _____ (v. 2)

Mary was _____ (v. 3)

This small but faithful family now understood the meaning of discipleship. They allowed God to use the personalities he had given them to be true devotees of his Son Jesus.

Martha was serving, but notice that she wasn't complaining. Lazarus was sitting with Jesus, making him feel welcome and at home. Mary was worshiping with her costly perfume and hair—outwardly expressing what she felt on the inside.

The effect this family had on their community was profound. Look at John 12:17 – 19 and write verse 19 below.

The Pharisees were totally frustrated in the aftermath of Lazarus's resurrection, enraged that the "whole world" was following after Jesus. This last line about shakes me off my seat because it illustrates that to this day, one man or woman committed to being a disciple of Jesus has the ability to turn the eyes of the world toward the Savior.

Our weapons are love and grace, not pushing or fighting. You can always tell a disciple by his or her authentic need for Jesus to be lifted up because nothing else really matters.

So, my friend, it is with a humble hug of grace that I leave you today. I hate good-byes more than I hate going to the dentist. I hope you know I'm not leaving for good, but just for a bit, until we sit at our Master's feet again to study. Please visit me at garimeacham.com or follow my mental meanderings on my blog trulyfed.blogspot.com.

I get to say what I've been dying to say since our first day together. "You've got guts!" And it's my honor to have taken this gutsy ride alongside you.

Hugs …

Gari

P.S. — I hope you're meeting one more week to discuss your personal study from Session 6 and to pray. I've included a bonus session guide for your time together. Blessings!

BONUS SESSION:
THE LOOK of a DISCIPLE

Session
Seven

GROUP DISCUSSION (approx. 30 minutes)

Discuss the following questions based on the week six personal study.

1. Why is the metaphor of potter and clay (Jeremiah 18:8; Romans 9:20–21) a perfect description for how God molds and uses us?

2. Even though the potter-and-clay metaphor sounds beautiful, it's anything but easy to swallow sometimes! How does the first pottery principle ring true in your life? (Pottery Principle #1: We don't want to be the clay; we want to be the potter.)

3. Given the life Daniel lived and the trials he faced, how do you think he viewed the first pottery principle?

4. How did King Nebuchadnezzar learn the ramifications of this principle, and the fact that he wasn't his own potter?

5. When Daniel's friends Shadrach, Meshach, and Abednego were about to be thrown into the furnace for their beliefs, they uttered some of the most mature words in the Bible:

   "If it be so, our God whom we serve is able to deliver us from the furnace of blazing fire; and He will deliver us out of your hand, O king. But even if He does not, let it be known to you, O king, that we are not going to serve your gods or worship the golden image that you have set up." (Daniel 3:17–18 NASB)

How is this response a sign of maturity? How does our faith line up with this type of declaration?

6. Some people (like Nebuchadnezzar) have to be pushed to a breaking point before they submit to the hand of God. Did you have a breaking point before you could hear and obey? Are you praying for someone to get to *their* breaking point? Explain.

7. Why is it easy to get stuck looking at the pot God is making other people into rather than focusing on the pot he is creating us to be? How can we remedy this?

8. How do you "fit into" 1 Peter 3:3–6 where Peter encourages women to think more about their internal beauty than their outward beauty? Is this a battle for you, or a cause for insecurity? Remember, Peter didn't say it's wrong to care about beauty, but only that a particular type of spirit is precious and beautiful to God.

9. What do you think of this statement from Day Four of the personal study: "In one of God's greatest ironies, though pain causes sorrow, that sorrow can cause growth if met with open surrender." How can sorrow cause growth if we let it?

10. What does a real disciple of Jesus look like to you? How can you tell a disciple from a fake?

11. What session of *Spirit Hunger* has been the most meaningful to you and why? How do you feel gutsier in your faith now that you have completed this study?

PRAYER FOCUS (approx. 30 minutes)

- Use the remainder of your time together to focus on prayer. If you can, dim the lights and quiet the environment. You may start by reflecting on Jesus' plea for us to ask, seek, and knock as we come to him.
- Think about the listening postures of humility and expectation. Sit quietly, humbly laying before God anything that might be in the way of your pure communication with him. Expectantly share with him what's on your hearts.
- If some participants would like to share their vision prayer, join one another in lifting those desires.
- As you close your time together, ask the Lord, "Where do we go from here?" What are his plans for you individually and as a group? Praise him for his presence in your weekly sessions and in your lives.

ACKNOWLEDGMENTS

I love reading authors' acknowledgments because I know that writing a book is much harder than it looks. It is a task that rivals childbirth, and the pains of my labor have been exceedingly helped by those I want to thank.

To Bobby—lover of my soul—I thank you for the countless talks and prayer and for the courage you exude that lets me tell your stories as well as my own.

To my children, Brooke, Ally, and Colton; and to my grandbaby, Reese— you are my joy and crown. I thank God for teaching me so much through you. I adore you.

To my dear friend Leanne Jamieson and the women of Second Baptist Church in Houston—thank you for taking this journey with me and letting me explore this material with you.

To my editors John Sloan and Dirk Buursma—you have taught me and mentored me with grace and encouragement. Thanks for your kindred spirit toward this work, and thanks for your gentle hand that led me through the pages.

To Cindy Lambert, Don Gates, Karin Tyrer, Robin Phillips, and the entire team at Zondervan—each hand this book has passed through has touched it with excellence. My thanks to you.

To the Zondervan DVD and curriculum team, including producer T. J. Rathbun and workbook editor Greg Clouse—thanks for your vision and cheerleading.

To Wendy Lawton, my agent and friend—thanks for speaking the words "for such a time as this …" over my life.

To my former students at Peabody Elementary School—I think I learned most of what I know about writing from you.

To my mom, sister, brother, dad, and grandparents—you are the bright mosaic of my life. I love you more than words can express.

To the people who work at Panera Bread—you always greeted me with a friendly smile and a large cup for me to fill with iced tea. I'm grateful.

To my friends in Major League Baseball—it is an honor to be part of this wonderful game with you all.

Finally, and most important—I thank my Savior, Jesus, who has saved, inspired, and rearranged my life. Without him I have no story to tell …

NOTES

1. Sue and Larry Richards, *Every Woman in the Bible* (Nashville: Thomas Nelson, 1999), 38.
2. Mark Batterson, *The Circle Maker* (Grand Rapids: Zondervan, 2011), 110.
3. Oswald Chambers, *The Quotable Oswald Chambers* (Grand Rapids: Discovery House, 2008), 176.
4. Lois Tverberg, *Walking in the Dust of Rabbi Jesus* (Grand Rapids: Zondervan, 2012), 118.
5. "Seven Reasons Not to Worry," *Life Application Bible* (Wheaton, Ill.: Tyndale House, 1988), 1338.
6. Tricia McCary Rhodes, *The Soul at Rest: A Journey into Contemplative Prayer* (Minneapolis: Bethany House, 1996), 208.
7. Oswald Chambers, *My Utmost for His Highest* (Uhrichsville, Ohio: Barbour, 2000), 53.
8. Robert J. Morgan, *On This Day in Christian History* (Nashville: Thomas Nelson, 1997), July 11.
9. Poem titled *Struggles in Life*, author unknown.
10. Richard Foster, *Prayer: Finding the Heart's True Home* (San Francisco: HarperSanFrancisco, 1992), 123.
11. Jim Cymbala, *Breakthrough Prayer* (Grand Rapids: Zondervan, 2003), 150.
12. Sue and Larry Richards, *Every Woman in the Bible*, 180.
13. *Every Woman in the Bible*, 181.
14. *Every Woman in the Bible*, 169.
15. Warren Wiersbe, *Be Compassionate* (Colorado Springs: David Cook, 1988), 126.
16. U.S. Department of State, *Seven Norms of Collaborative Work*, posted on www.state.gov/m/a/os/43984.htm.
17. John C. Maxwell, *Running with the Giants* (New York: Faith Words, Hachette Book Group, 2002), 101-102.
18. Robert Morgan, *On This Day in Christian History*, July 24.
19. *On This Day in Christian History*, October 15.
20. Andy Stanley, *Visioneering* (Colorado Springs: Multnomah, 1999), 17.
21. *Life Application Bible*, 1192.
22. *Life Application Bible*, 1933.
23. Oswald Chambers, *My Utmost for His Highest*, 127.

Spirit Hunger
Filling Our Deep Longing to Connect with God

Gari Meacham

We all have a desperate need for God—not just for following him or being committed to him, but to be intimately connected to him.

We long for purpose, for affirmation, for attention, for nurture. But Gari Meacham writes that we fall short of being desperate for God, or we miss the longed-for romance with God we hear about in Scripture. We're uncertain how to distinguish our longings from our fears. When, says Meacham, did our longings turn to hauntings? And when did we buy into the counterfeit yearnings for control, and the insecurity, perfectionism and other attitudes that quench Spirit Hunger?

The answer to Spirit Hunger is to engage God like never before. In this book Meacham shows through her story and the stories of others how to turn worry into belief, problems, and heartaches into a life of intimate prayer, and sighs for intimacy into closeness with God. She discusses her discoveries about prayer, including why asking is sometimes hard, how we can notice and track God's movements as we seek his answers, and why it's sometimes such a struggle to believe after we've prayed.

Meacham writes, "With the authenticity of my own life stories—marriage to a professional baseball player, struggles with severe food bondage, and a father who was a quadriplegic—I came to the crisp realization that my prayer life and my belief needed to match. *Spirit Hunger* provides a clear path toward matching these heart cries—leading away from crumbs and counterfeit to a hungering for God."

Available in stores and online!